Proclaiming the Good News

in the Heart of Missouri

Loretta Pastva, SND

THE CATHOLIC DIOCESE OF JEFFERSON CITY,

MISSOURI

❧ *His Holiness Pope Benedict XVI*

(Photo credit: L'Osservatore Romano)

❧ *Bishop John R. Gaydos*

WITH A SHEPHERD'S CARE

Letter from the Bishop

Dear Friends in Christ,

It gives me great joy as the Bishop of Jefferson City to mark the jubilee celebration of the 50th Anniversary of the founding of the Diocese by His Holiness, Pope Pius XII. As we look back over the past fifty years, there is certainly much for which we can be grateful to God. We give thanks for our predecessors who first brought the Catholic faith to northeastern and central Missouri from far-flung corners of the globe. We are grateful for the sacrifices and dedication of so many bishops, priests, religious, deacons and laity who built the network of parishes, schools and institutions we see today, united together with His Holiness, Pope Benedict XVI.

In particular, I want to express my own appreciation to Sister Loretta Pastva, SND for this eminently readable history of our Local Church. I also wish to acknowledge the publishers, Les Éditions du Signe in Strasbourg, France, for their artistry in presenting so much of the beauty to be found in our 38-county Diocese. It is my hope that the story of the life of the Roman Catholic Church in this section of Missouri will become better known through their efforts.

THE CATHOLIC DIOCESE OF JEFFERSON CITY, MISSOURI

4

In this history of our first fifty years, we discover anew that witness of solid faith which encourages us to embrace the present with Gospel love and to walk into our future with unwavering hope. Keeping before us the witness of these diocesan ancestors and strengthened by the prayerful intercession of the Immaculate Heart of Mary, our diocesan patroness, we move ahead, together weaving the continuation of our diocesan history. The Risen Jesus accompanies us on our way and enables us to recognize him, as the disciples of Emmaus did, 'in the breaking of the bread' (Lk 24:35). May Jesus find us watchful, ready to recognize his face and running to our brothers and sisters with the good news: 'We have seen the Lord' (Jn 20:25).

With my best wishes and personal regards for each of you and your families, I am

Sincerely yours in Christ,

+ John R. Gaydos

Most Reverend John R. Gaydos
Bishop of Jefferson City

Author/Editor
Loretta Pastva, SND

Resources
Our Story: 1957-1984
Diocesan Archives
Parish Archives

Consultants
Most Reverend John R. Gaydos, Honorary Chair
Reverend Robert A. Kurwicki, Chair
Sister Peggy Bonnot, CCVI
Reverend William D. Debo
Ms. Janet Hernandez
Mr. Jay Nies
Mr. Mark S. Saucier
Mrs. Annette Smith
Deacon John D. Weaver

Photography
John Glover

Published by
Éditions du Signe
B.P. 94 - 67038 Strasbourg – Cedex 2 – France
Tel (+33) 388 789 191
Fax (+33) 388 789 199
info@editionsdusigne.fr

Publishing Director
Christian Riehl

Director of Publication
Joëlle Bernhard

Publishing Assistant
Marc de Jong

Design and Layout
Juliette Roussel

Photoengraving
Éditions du Signe DB - 106465

© Éditions du Signe 2005
ISBN: 2-7468-1521-4

Table of Contents

Diocese of Jefferson City

Unionville
Memphis
Wayland
Kahoka
St. Patrick
Milan
Kirksville
Baring
Canton
Novinger
LaGrange
Edina
Ewing
Brookfield
Bevier
Palmyra
Marceline
Shelbina
Hannibal
Hurricane
Branch
Macon
Wein
Monroe City
Indian Grove
Indian Creek
Perry
Brunswick
Salisbury
Moberly
Paris
Louisiana
Slater
Vandalia
St. Clement
Clarksville
Marshall
Glasgow
Mexico
Laddonia
Centralia
Martinsburg
Wellsville
Sweet Springs
Fayette
Columbia
Boonville
Montgomery City
Sedalia
Pilot Grove
Fulton
Jonesburg
Holts
Mokane
Rhineland
Summit
Hermann
California
7
Morrison
1
8
Bahner
Tipton
Jefferson
9
City
2
10
11
3
13
12
Versailles
4
15
Eldon
5
Cole Camp
16
19
Laurie
6
14
18
Warsaw
Mary's Home
Vienna
Owensville
Belle
Bourbon
St. Elizabeth
Rosati
Climax
Brinktown
Cuba
Springs
St. Anthony
St. James
Hermitage
Dixon
Steelville
Camdenton
Crocker
Rolla
Richland
St. Robert

KEY FOR COLE & OSAGES COUNTIES:

1. St. Martin
2. Taos
3. Russellville
4. Wardsville
5. Osage Bend
6. St. Thomas
7. Chamois
8. Frankenstein
9. Bonnots Mill
10. Loose Creek
11. Linn
12. Rich Fountain
13. Folk
14. Meta
15. Westphalia
16. Koeltztown
17. Freeburg
18. Argyle

Sources of a Renewed Church

It was 1956 and it looked like summer moving into bountiful harvest in the Church in America. Everything was thriving after the war that followed "the war to end all wars." World War II General Dwight D. Eisenhower was elected to guide the nation in the post war years. The GI Bill had provided many returning soldiers with the means to higher education and they were now making their way up the ladder of success. Political office-holders were seeing more Catholics among their ranks. Catholic churches were in view on every other corner. Catholic school attendance was at a peak and vocations to the priesthood and religious life flourished as never before in the history of the Faith.

CHANGING DEMOGRAPHY

But right around the corner, chill winds were circling. European immigrants in the late 19th century had arrived en masse from their respective homelands and clustered in neighborhoods around their churches to protect and nurture the languages, customs and traditions of the "old country." Now, many who had grown up in the cities found themselves drawn to the outskirts of the urban centers, breaking up the ethnic enclaves created by the mass movement to the cities during the Industrial Revolution that followed the Civil War. In the mid-fifties, Catholic Christians found themselves daily rubbing shoulders with people of different persuasions in sprawling suburbs created by their flight from the ghettoes. The Supreme Court's decision to desegregate public transportation in the Rosa Parks case fanned the fires of the Civil Rights Movement.

Change charged Catholicism throughout the world as under the benign and expansive reign of Pope Pius XII (1939-1958) biblical and liturgical scholars in Europe and America were permitted to pursue studies that had been forbidden by Pius X (1903-1914) in his desperate attempt to stave off the disease of "modernism" that seemed to threaten the Faith. The pressing questions of the day had shifted from how to defend the faith against the onslaughts of heretics to how to coexist amicably and fruitfully in a modern world fashioned by new philosophies, unprecedented leaps in scientific knowledge and global communication. And with change came new life.

ᕔ *Bishop Joseph M. Marling, C.PP.S., greets the faithful at his installation Mass as founding Bishop of Jefferson City in 1956.*

VATICAN II

It was against this background that the Dioceses of Jefferson City, Kansas City-St. Joseph and Springfield-Cape Girardeau were born in 1956. Only six years after the reorganization of the Ecclesiastical Province of St. Louis, the successor of Pius XII, Blessed John XXIII, set in motion a plan to open the windows of the universal Church. By launching Vatican Council II, he aimed to pour light and Spirit into a Church that for too long had been defensively shielding itself from secular society. For centuries it had been relying more on form than substance, valuing legalism over personal commitment to Jesus Christ and in need of reawakening of its mission to promote social justice and respect for the consciences of others.

Suddenly where there had been no change for 700 years, certainly not after the reactionary Councils of Trent (1545) and Vatican I (1870), new insights, new practices, new theologies and a new Catholicism were born. Even the liturgical language that had seemed to unite the Church all over the world

ᗯ *Archbishop Karl J. Alter of Cincinnati and Bishop Joseph M. Marling C.PP.S.of Jefferson City on the steps of St. Peter's Basilica prior to entering a session of the Second Vatican Council in 1963.* (Photo by Giordani)

was replaced by the use of national tongues. It was the springtime promised by the prophets of the early decades of the century.

Bishop Joseph Mary Marling, C.PP.S., the first chief shepherd of the newly formed northcentral diocese held a steady course in the face of the swirling waters upon which the Church sailed in the early aftermath of the Council. Reserved in manner, and not one to adopt every new fad, he was nevertheless loyal to Church teaching as expressed in the decrees of the Council. He began at once to implement the changes called for by the Council. Building on the efforts of those who preceded him and setting the course for the future, he brought the local Church of Jefferson City safely through the agony and ecstasy of a historic period before his resignation in 1969.

ᗯ *Bishop Joseph M. Marling C.PP.S. of Jefferson City, serving as president of the National Catholic Rural Life Conference, addresses the 1960 NCRLC convention in Jefferson City.*

ONE:

Before We Came to Be 1539-1956

"You will show me the path to life."

Psalm 16:11

Early Adventurers

Although the diocese was brand new and set in an era of rapid change, the Church in the northcentral area of Missouri was far from being in its infancy. There was a Catholic presence from the beginning. The early years of the 16th century saw Spanish and French adventurers setting sail to gain lands in the New World for their countries of origin and their kings. The Spaniard Fernando De Soto was reputedly the first white man to set foot in Missouri. With an expedition of some 720 men, he moved inland from the western coast of Florida in 1539 in search of riches in the new country. When he reached the Great River two years later, he claimed the entire Mississippi Valley for Catholic Spain. His band included 12 Spanish priests, 8 brothers and 4 monks who instructed the friendlier of the Indians that Christians are immortal. Crossing the Mississippi a little south of present Memphis, he and his companions turned northward on the west bank to the present Caruthersville, Missouri.

In 1673 Father James Marquette and layman entrepreneurs like Pierre Laclede Liguest and Clerk Augur Choteau passed through the area to learn whether the Great River emptied into the Gulf of Mexico. A hundred and fifty years later, the French Catholic explorer Robert Cavelier Sieur de la Salle, murdered in ambush five years afterwards on April 19, 1682, planted the French fleur de lis on the banks of the Mississippi in the conviction that claiming the river gained for France the rights to the

Hernando De Soto directs the raising of a large cross designating the territory a possession of Spain.

(Used by permission, State Historical Society of Missouri, Columbia)

lands it drained. He opened the way for French Catholics to be instrumental in the settlement of the land, and they came in droves to work the mines and establish trading posts on the western banks of the Mississippi. But it wasn't until almost 30 years after the French set up the first fur trading stations at Ste. Genevieve in 1735 and a little later at St. Louis that the first mission and permanent settlements appeared in 1764. The first church was built in 1770.

The wide, though muddy, Missouri River and its tributaries formed roads that encouraged movement ever onward. No doubt the main driving force behind the adventurers was business opportunity, yet the people from Tennessee and Virginia as well as from Germany, Ireland and Scotland who followed brought their Catholic faith with them and lived according to its values.

But the French and Indian War (1754-1763) was to disrupt the Mississippi River society. With the French looking only to peaceful settlement, the British intent upon claiming the Ohio Valley and the Spanish allied with the French, the war resulted in the British forcing France to cede all her North American territorial possessions east of the Mississippi and north of Ohio, including Canada. Louis XV, pressed for funds, gave over "Louisiana"-- "all the land west of the Mississippi claimed by France," in the Treaty of Fontainebleau (1762) to Spain. With the transfer, the 100-year ecclesiastical jurisdiction passed from the French Bishop of Quebec to the Spanish Bishop of Havana, Cuba. Eight years later, Spain returned the Louisiana Territory to France by secret treaty.

MISSOURI is named for the tribe that inhabited the area with the Osage and Caddoan people. Both were farmers, but were strongly influenced by the nomadic bison hunters of the Great Plains. DeSoto arrived in 1541. The first Anglo settlement was established at Ste. Genevieve in 1741. The territory became part of the United States at the Louisiana Purchase in 1803. Three trails, through Santa Fe, Oregon and Colorado, threaded through Kansas City and Independence. In 1821, Missouri was admitted to the Union as a slave-holding state. Eventually, it sided with the Union in the Civil War. Its central location as a crossroads on the north-south trade route and the east-west railroad lines gave the state commercial importance. Today Missouri is a leading manufacturing and food-processing state with stockyards in Kansas City and service industries, agriculture, mining and tourism forming its main sources of commerce.

Ecclesiastical Jurisdictions

With these and other territorial transfers east of the Mississippi from Canada to the Gulf, questions of diocesan jurisdictions arose among the Catholic settlers. In the early 1760s, only one priest, Fr. Sebastian Louis Meurin, served all of "Upper Louisiana." Upon Meurin's death in 1777, Fr. Pierre Gibault, who defended the people's moral right to submit to the rule of the new United States, found himself the lone pastor in the vast area. In his declining years, his bishop in Canada, who was disenchanted by Gibault's support for the American cause, forbade him to return there.

At the request of the governor of Louisiana, Estevan Miro, Gibault was appointed to serve in New Madrid in 1789. The cypress-timbered church and rectory, which were subsidized by

the Spanish government, were washed away in the cataclysmic earthquakes of 1811 and 1812.

෴ *Window celebrating the Eucharist, St. Anthony, Camdenton*

In 1755 Pierre Liguest Laclède, a French nobleman, came to Louisiana seeking to engage in commerce in New Orleans. His company, Maxent, Laclède and Company, became the sole negotiators with the Northwest Indians. But the Treaty of Parish (1763) ended the company's privilege and ceded Louisiana--all the territory from the Gulf of Mexico to Canada and from the Mississippi to the Rocky Mountains--to Spain. Laclède bought out his partners and settled west of the Mississippi, giving rise to the city now known as St. Louis.

With Spain's accession, all of the Louisiana territory came under the jurisdiction of the Diocese of Santiago de Cuba (1759-1787). Frenchman Fr. Luke Collet, a Recollect, and Fr. Sebastian Louis Meurin, who built the first church in 1766, were the pioneer priests living among the people. The Capuchin Fathers arrived for service in 1772.

Hard pressed for funds, Napoleon persuaded Spain in 1800 to cede the territory back to France and in 1803 sold it to the Union for $15 million. The vast territory of what was then known as Louisiana came under several ecclesiastical jurisdictions.

Lands East of the Mississippi
- 1658-1674 Vicariate Apostolic of Canada
- 1674-1784 Diocese of Quebec, Canada
- 1784-1789 Prefecture Apostolic of 13 States of the Union
- 1789-1808 Bishop of Baltimore, Maryland
- 1808-1834 Diocese of Bardstown, Kentucky

Lands West of the Mississippi
- 1658-1674   Vicariate Apostolic of Canada
- 1674-1759 Diocese of Quebec, Canada
- 1759-1787 Diocese of Santiago de Cuba
- 1787-1793 Diocese of Havana, Cuba
- 1793-1826 Diocese of Louisiana and the Floridas (St. Louis of New Orleans)

In July 1826, St. Louis was separated from the Diocese of Louisiana, which changed its name to Diocese of New Orleans. The borders of the new diocese were Canada on the north; the western boundaries of Washington State, Oregon and part of Nevada on the west; the northern borders of Arizona, New Mexico, Texas and Louisiana on the South; and half of Wisconsin and Illinois on the east. St. Louis was raised to an Archdiocese July 20, 1847.

By 1868 the Diocese of St. Joseph was carved out of the Archdiocese of Louisiana with Bishop John Joseph Hogan appointed as Ordinary. It encompassed the northwestern corner of Missouri between the Missouri and the Chariton Rivers changing the boundary of St. Louis to Canada on the north, Kansas on the West, the northern border of Arkansas on the south and the Mississippi River on the east. The Diocese of St. Joseph was to remain a separate jurisdiction until 1893.

In September 1880, the lands south of the Missouri River and west of the eastern boundary of Moniteau, Miller, Camden, Laclede, Wright, Douglass and Ozark counties were established as the Diocese of Kansas City. Bishop Hogan from St. Joseph became the Ordinary while retaining administration of the Diocese of St. Joseph.

In 1911, 12 counties above the Missouri north of St. Louis were added to the Diocese of St. Joseph.

Finally on July 2, 1956, the state of Missouri was divided into three suffragan dioceses under the jurisdiction of the metropolitan Archdiocese of St. Louis. The Diocese of Springfield-Cape Girardeau was established in the southern third of the state. The Diocese of Jefferson City, created from Kansas City, St. Joseph and St. Louis, extended to the north and central portions. And St. Joseph was united to Kansas City's 27 counties to encompass the north and western Diocese of Kansas City - St. Joseph.

👁 *Stained-glass window of the Nativity*

Between 1787 and 1818, clusters of Catholic families of French, Irish and German extraction settled just beyond the western bank of the Mississippi and 80 miles south of St. Louis. Originally known as the Barrens Colony, it would in time be renamed Perryville after the

naval hero of the War of 1812, Oliver Hazard Perry. Beginning in 1790, the Colony was served by an Irish priest trained in Spain, Fr. James Maxwell.

When Fr. Louis William Valentine DuBourg was named Bishop of Louisiana in 1815, he established his See in St. Louis, Upper Louisiana, and the Diocese of St. Louis was erected in 1826. Its boundaries encompassed Wisconsin, Illinois and "everything west of the Mississippi." The parish at Fredericktown was established in 1827.

Pope Pius VII heeded the pleas of Bishop Du Bourg for priests for his flock and promised to establish a seminary in Cape Girardeau, to be run by the Congregation of the Mission. When Fr. Joseph Rosati arrived at the Barrens in 1818 with a team of Vincentians, they located their house there, despite bitter religious prejudice in the Cape. The seminary formed numerous Vincentian missionaries whose impact on the growth of the Catholic Church reached not only to Missouri, but south to Texas and northern Mexico and west to California. At the request of Fr. Rosati, who later followed Bishop Du Bourg to become the first Bishop of St. Louis, the Sisters of Loretto opened St. Vincent Women's Academy in 1838.

Scots-Irish

The Americains, as the French and Spanish called the migrants from the eastern United States, began to swell the population of Missouri beginning in the 1790s. Originating in Scotland, their ancestors had migrated to Northern Ireland during the 1600s after the English Civil War that had decidedly put down the Roman Catholic influence in England. Drawn by William Penn's policies of freedom of religion in the New World, the Scots-Irish arrived in droves to Pennsylvania. As frontiers moved westward, they moved with them

through Virginia, Tennessee and Kentucky, eventually reaching Missouri. They brought with them their old prejudices, superstitions and suspicion of all things French, including the Catholic Church and tended to work hard, keep to themselves and distrust the government.

Their freedom-loving, independent and self-reliant spirit clashed with the spirit of docile obedience to ecclesiastical superiors that marked their Catholic neighbors who had come under the influence of the well-educated

French Jesuits. Rugged individualists, the Scots-Irish favored separation of Church and state. Incidents of vandalism and the rise of movements like the anti-Catholic Nativists political party marked the later 1800s, discouraging efforts at evangelization.

Development Westward

The Louisiana Purchase of 1803 almost doubled the size of the new republic and opened the door to the interior of the land. Lewis and Clarke pushed out from St. Louis to find a route to the Pacific and with the War of 1812 the United States defeated the British who were interfering with movement westward. Within less than 20 years of the Louisiana Purchase, in 1820, Missouri was admitted to statehood as the young U.S. government tried through the Missouri Compromise to keep the nation together by balancing the number of free and slave states.

Land expansion was the watchword for the States during the 19th Century. In the same year as the first capital building in Jefferson City was built, the Monroe Doctrine forbade future colonization by foreign countries. The completion of the Erie Canal linked the Hudson with Lake Erie in 1825. Three years

ॐ *Window of Saints, Shrine of St. Patrick, St. Patrick*

later, construction on the B & O railroad began. The population of Missouri grew from 20,845 in 1810 to 3,293,335 in 1910. Texas became independent of Mexico in 1836 to be annexed to the young nation in 1845. The Treaty of Guadalupe Hidalgo in 1840 added Mexican California to the States. A little later, Spain was to cede control of Puerto Rico, Guam and the Philippines to the U.S. Hawaii and Samoa were annexed in 1898.

Central Location

Missouri's location in the physical center of the U.S. landmass heightened its importance to the Union. When the Confederacy of Southern States was formed in 1861 to fight the emancipation of slaves, Missouri remained on the side of the Union, although at least half its population was sympathetic to the South. Hadn't the Dred Scott decision of 1857 handed down from a St. Louis courthouse declared that a slave was property and not free to move to a free state? Four years after the end of the Civil War, in 1869, the first transcontinental railroad joined the Central Pacific and the Union Pacific and Missouri became the gateway to the West.

St. Joseph, Missouri, was the starting point of the remarkable feat of the Pony Express. Some 180 men participated for 18 months from 1860-1861 to keep the mail service between St. Joseph and Sacramento going day and night. The Santa Fe and Oregon Trails began in Independence, Missouri. The world-renowned Gateway Arch in St. Louis, begun in 1963, rising 630 feet, symbolized the pivotal role of Missouri in the Westward movement. And although masses were to pass through, many Irish and German immigrants decided to make Missouri their home. The population of Missouri came to be comprised of these as well as of adventurers and freed slaves.

Father Ferdinand Helias S. J.

1817-1874

FATHER Ferdinand Helias D'Huddghem, founder of seven parishes in the present-day Jefferson City diocese, is known as the Apostle of Central Missouri.

Born into an aristocratic family in 1796 in Belgium, he entered the Society of Jesus (the Jesuits) in 1817, was ordained to the holy priesthood in 1825, and traveled to the United States in 1833 to serve as a missionary. He spent two years in Pennsylvania, then moved to St. Louis to teach at Saint Louis University and serve a German-speaking congregation that would become St. Joseph parish. He was sent to central Missouri in 1838 to minister to the German immigrants in and around Westphalia. From there, he established missions in Rich Fountain, Jefferson City, Cedron, St. Thomas, Loose Creek, and Taos, which became and would remain his home until his death in 1874. Those missions grew into parishes, and out of those and the rest of the territory he visited on horseback were carved an additional 22, most of which remain in service.

Early on, Fr. Helias established a mission circuit, offering Mass in homes of isolated Catholics and baptizing their children. He also established Catholic ministry to the incarcerated, offering the first Mass at the old Missouri State Penitentiary in around 1838.

He continued to serve as the area's population grew and other priests were sent to help him care for their souls. Having endured the discomforts of a pioneer existence and been obliged to defend the Faith on many occasions, he asked his superiors for permission to remain in Missouri as he got older and his health began to deteriorate. He died of a stroke outside the old St. Francis Xavier Church in Taos on Aug. 11, 1874, on his way to ring the bell for the Angelus. His remains were buried in the Taos parish cemetery and were moved almost 90 years later to a granite crypt in the church vestibule. The top of the stone altar, donated by his mother, from the church he built now marks the place of his death outside the present church in

This painting of Jesuit Father Ferdinand Helias, known as the "Apostle of Central Missouri" for his work in establishing and cultivating Catholicism in this area from the 1830s until his death in 1874, belongs to St. Peter parish in Jefferson City.

Taos. On it is inscribed a passage from the Book of Genesis: "Go forth from the land of your kinsfolk and from your father's house to a land that I will show you."

The Catholic high school in Jefferson City bears his name, as does one of that city's two Knights of Columbus councils.

The fruit of his missionary endeavors has been remarkably enduring. The area in which he primarily served has remained largely Catholic, with Osage County in particular having the largest percentage of people identifying themselves as members of Holy Mother Church in the entire state.

HELIAS INTERPARISH HIGH SCHOOL, JEFFERSON CITY

HISTORY: Through the combined efforts of the clergy and people of Jefferson City, Helias Interparish High School opened its doors for the 1956-57 school year to the youth of central Missouri.

This interparish Catholic school became necessary when St. Peter High School (built in 1930) was sorely overtaxed by the WWII baby boom population in this area. Named after Jesuit missionary Father Ferdinand Helias, the school was designed for 600 students and was located on Swifts Highway. It was staffed by the Christian Brothers, School Sisters of Notre Dame, Diocesan Priests and lay women and men. Until 1969, Helias was co-institutional, meaning that the boys and girls had no classes together. The Sisters taught the girls, and the Brothers taught the boys. In 1971 James L. Rackers was named the first layman to direct a Catholic school. Today over 900 students are served by an administrative team headed by Dennis Hughes and an especially dedicated faculty. After a half-century of service, Helias now boasts more than 7,000 graduates.

Bishop John R. Gaydos in August 2004 presided at a Mass to open the school's yearlong golden jubilee celebration. "As we come to the Altar this day," said Bishop Gaydos, "we come recognizing all the people who have benefited from the great grace that is Helias High School, and we also are very eager that this mission, this grace will continue to grow, to enrich our community, to enrich our world, but most importantly will continue to be a reflection of the glory of God."

MISSOURI STATE PENITENTIARY: FIRST AND LAST EUCHARIST

JESUIT Father Ferdinand Helias, known as the Apostle of Central Missouri, reportedly celebrated the first Mass in the Missouri State Penitentiary in Jefferson City around 1838. When the prison — which opened in 1836 and over time became the oldest operating corrections facility west of the Mississippi River — was closed and replaced with a new facility in 2004, Bishop John R. Gaydos of Jefferson City celebrated the last Mass in a chapel not far from the site of Fr. Helias' first Mass. The Altar stone from the MSP chapel has been made a part of the new Altar in the St. Alphonsus Ligouri Chapel at the Alphonse J. Schwartze Memorial Catholic Center. "Every time we have Mass there, it will remind us of his prayer for the people in prison and those who have died there," said Father Joseph S. Corel, Catholic chaplain of the old prison when it closed, and currently of the new one.

❧ *Bishop John R. Gaydos celebrates the last Mass in the All Faiths Chapel at the old Missouri State Penitentiary in Jefferson City, shortly before the prison was closed and replaced. With him is Father Joseph S. Corel, Catholic chaplain at the prison. About 166 years previously, Jesuit Father Ferdinand Helias celebrated what was believed to be the first Mass at the prison.*

FATHER AUGUSTINE TOLTON
1854-1897

TWO African slaves named Peter and Martha Tolton were married in Ralls County, Mo., and had three children, all baptized in the old St. Peter Church in Brush Creek near Monroe City in the present-day Jefferson City diocese. Their second son, Augustine, was born in 1854. Peter Tolton went to St. Louis to fight for the Union in the Civil War and died of dysentery.

Martha Tolton and her children either escaped or were freed and crossed the Mississippi River at Hannibal into Illinois, a free state. The family continued to practice their Catholic faith while living in Quincy, Ill., where Augustine (also known as Augustus) began to feel called to the priesthood. Priests at local parishes and nearby St. Francis Solanus College (now Quincy University) helped him study, but no American seminary or religious community would admit him. Eventually, he was accepted into the Urban College (now Urbanian University) of the Propagation of the Faith in Rome, hoping to become a missionary in Africa. He was ordained to the priesthood in 1886 in the Basilica of St. John Lateran in Rome, and celebrated his Mass of Thanksgiving in St. Peter's Basilica. Realizing an opportunity to help Catholics and all people of faith in the United States overcome racial prejudice, the Society for the Propagation of the Faith sent Fr. Tolton back to Quincy to serve, making him the first full-blooded African-American priest to be recognized in the United States. He and many of his African-American congregants eventually moved to Chicago, where they established the Mission of St. Monica, serving some of the city's poorest residents. He died of heat exhaustion in 1897, at age 43, and his remains are buried in St. Peter Catholic Cemetery in Quincy. The present St. Peter Church in Brush Creek, currently undergoing restoration, was built in 1862 and has not been used as a parish church since 1966, although Masses are celebrated there twice a year. Holy Rosary parish in nearby Monroe City hosted a Mass in 2004 to celebrate the 150th anniversary of Fr. Tolton's birth. There, descendants of the family that had claimed ownership of the Toltons worshiped with descendants of Fr. Tolton's extended family. The emphasis was on reconciliation and the courage Fr. Tolton had showed in living out his priestly vocation. "Neither brilliant nor clever," said Jesuit Father J. Glen Murray, guest homilist, "America's first recognized black African-American priest was a pastor, first and last, and justly merits the title of father of all the black African-American priests and — dare I say — the father of all black African-Americans who labor in love in the Catholic Church."

Father Augustine Tolton, also known as Augustus, is pictured in an undated photo. Born a plantation slave in northeastern Missouri, he was ordained a priest April 24, 1886, in Rome, where he said his First Mass at St. Peter's Basilica the next day.

Bishop John J. Hogan

1829-1913

BISHOP John J. Hogan was a horseback missionary in northern Missouri and eventually became founding bishop of two dioceses. A native of Limerick, Ireland, he served first in southern Missouri parishes, then in the late 1850s and early '60s served a 32-county area (roughly the size of his native country) that had no resident priest. He established the missions that today are the parishes of Macon, Milan, Brookfield, Brunswick, Mexico, Moberly and Martinsburg in the present-day Jefferson City diocese, as well as the Chillicothe, Sturgeon and Cameron parishes, now in the Kansas City-St. Joseph Diocese, and said Mass and administered the sacraments in the homes of many Catholics who had access to no other priests.

He had grown up dreaming about the excitement of preaching in the missions on the Great Plains of the United States. One of his favorite images in the Society for the Propagation of the Faith's illustrated magazines was of the old St. Louis Cathedral.

Early in his missionary career, on the back of his tired horse, he predicted to a well-dressed Protestant astride a majestic stallion in northern Missouri that one day, there would be a Catholic church on every hill there. The man replied derisively, "Yes — when the Chariton River flows upstream."

Bishop Hogan was an ardent supporter of the Union during the Civil War and narrowly missed being killed in the Chillicothe Massacre. According to his memoirs, Confederate-sympathizing guerrillas captured him and were seconds from executing him when a man named Jesse James told them not to shoot because he was a priest.

After the Civil War, he was indicted for preaching without taking an oath of allegiance to the Union, as was required under the Missouri Constitution of 1865. Rather than meeting the sheriff at the courthouse and quietly posting bond, he donned his clerical garb, picked up his

☙ *Bishop John J. Hogan founded many Catholic missions in northern Missouri before serving as founding Bishop of St. Joseph in 1868, then founding Bishop of Kansas City in 1880.*

crucifix and Bible, and accompanied the sheriff ceremoniously on foot. He was released pending trial, and the charges were dropped when the U.S. Supreme Court ruled the oath requirement invalid.

Pope Pius IX in 1868 appointed him founding bishop of the old St. Joseph Diocese, and Pope Leo XIII in 1880 appointed him founding bishop of the old Kansas City diocese. Bishop Hogan built two cathedrals and helped establish the Conception Abbey, where monks at Conception Seminary College educate most college seminarians for this diocese.

The dioceses he founded are now part of the present-day Jefferson City, Kansas City-St. Joseph and Springfield-Cape Girardeau dioceses, all established in 1956.

New Waves of Immigration

The establishment of Ellis Island at the beginning of the 19th century as the entry port for immigrants brought in many Eastern European peoples — Italians, Bohemians, Czechs and Slovaks — all Catholic. The poor Irish who had lacked property and opportunity to hone political skills in the homeland and had endured trying conditions during years of famine came starry eyed but unprepared to their new environment.

In the late 1800s, the influx of Catholic German immigrants of the 1830s and 1840s and the Irish immigrants of the late 1800s that swelled the population in the nation as a whole made its mark on the demography of the state of Missouri. Newcomers, especially from Alsace, brought with them a sturdy faith and their European expressions of it. Finding the price of land in Ohio at $5 an acre out of reach, they moved on to Missouri where land in places went for $1.25 an acre. By 1858, German Catholics were building their own churches.

Fertile land, availability of water, and abundance of trees and open spaces attracted people on the move. At the same time, the risks and dangers of the pioneer life developed qualities that promoted in the people an awareness of the needs of others and concern for the land and its resources, qualities that characterize the people yet today. If for many years the Church of Missouri came under the heading of Mission territory, in the middle of the 20th century reliance on European gifts disappeared. Rome recognized the maturing of the diocese by changing its jurisdiction from Propagation of the Faith to Congregation for the Evangelization of Peoples. Missourians had progressed with the Church from being recipients of mission to people of mission to others.

🙠 *Stained glass window of Creation at Our Lady of Lourdes, Columbia*

The Catholics living in north and mid central Missouri in the days before Jefferson City became a separate diocese had experienced World War II, the building of the Panama Canal, the first long distance telephone service and the first transatlantic flight. Before the Diocese was to be carved out, the stock market crashed, World War II resulted in the defeat of Germany, the Marshall Plan was put into effect, NATO, the UN, the Korean War and McCarthyism became household words.

TWO:

A Vibrant New Diocese 1956-1984

"...that they might have life and have it to the full."

John 10:10

Although the Catholics of Missouri had been practicing their faith for many decades before, the establishment of the Diocese of Jefferson City gave them a new sense of identity. The first 25 years were a time for both looking back and looking ahead.

Coming of Age

Whereas in times past missionaries often served the area, now a flurry of new churches, schools, rectories and convents was called for as the state experienced phenomenal growth in the decade between 1956 and 1966. The Baby Boom following the war, advances in technology, expansion of industry, changes in rural life and in patterns of leisure time activities brought about shifts in demography and, to some extent, culture. The Church in Missouri was to experience the birth pangs of coming of age.

The new diocese gladly took responsibility for its own expenses and spiritual development. The response was more than might have been expected. Besides assuming the cost of many new building projects, the people generously established and supported missions in Peru.

In fact, the diocese at mid-century had the highest percentage of priests serving in the missions and per capita giving to the missions was the highest in the nation.

Stained-glass window of the Word of God as two-edged sword at SS Peter and Paul Church, Boonville

Not without Cost

Consolidation did not come about all at once, however. With the resources and personnel of the larger St. Louis Archdiocese, Diocese of Kansas City and Diocese of St. Joseph now largely curtailed and the sparser population of the heartland, the new diocese had to fall back on its own gifts. The laity were asked to embrace the sacrifices attendant upon financing their new places of worship and education. The priests had to come to terms with the pain of separation from priests they had known and with whom they had trained. Clergy from St. Joseph, Kansas City and St. Louis now found themselves in new associations, and it was

⌖ As metropolitan archbishop of St. Louis from 1946-67, Joseph Cardinal Ritter was a spiritual father of the neighboring Jefferson City Diocese.

obvious from the start that the laity would be asked to assume greater involvement in church ministries and activities. Accordingly, there was a corresponding need to develop skills for broader participation. To deal with these eventualities, the diocese immediately launched out on its own creative projects and processes.

Parish and diocesan listening sessions were set up. The aim was to awaken stewardship and leadership among the people in the pews. These sessions resulted in a program to give a deeper sense of the meaning of the Church and the role of each person as a part of the world community to continue the work of Jesus. Other efforts that worked to inaugurate a new spirit in the fledgling diocese included the Stewardship Renewal Program, clergy retreats for updating and uniting the ordained ministers, the Priests Senate and the formation of a Diocesan Pastoral Council.

Effects of the Council

Vatican II both confirmed the vibrant life evident in the diocese and caused confusion. The new approaches to worship and to people of other denominations incurred exhilaration and resistance, polarizing groups. Bishop Marling and Bishop McAuliffe introduced and used the theme of death and resurrection to give meaning to the letting go

that was required for the agenda of renewal to take hold. Conversion and metanoia became household words in the "Direction: 80s" process as on the diocesan as well as the parochial levels efforts were made to work together to find a balance between stagnation and excess. Follow-up programs reinforced the movement forward.

Pope John Paul II's 1979 visit to Des Moines, Iowa, addressing concerns for the resource of the land was especially influential. It drew many from the diocese, especially farmers struggling in the face of changing conditions in agriculture. The diocese experienced an upsurge in social consciousness as by education and lobbying the Missouri Catholic Conference strove to influence the passing of laws to protect the farmers.

⌖ Pope John Paul II greets Bishop Michael F. McAuliffe during the Pope's visit to Denver in 1993.

A DEEPLY spiritual, holy priest of the Society of the Most Precious Blood, Bishop Joseph M. Marling was the founding bishop of the Diocese of Jefferson City and its chief shepherd from 1956 to 1969. He was born on August 31, 1904, in Centralia, West Virginia, the second son of John and Sarah F. (O'Neill) Marling. His father was a cabinetmaker and his mother, born in Ireland, came to the United States at age 18. He attended St. Joseph School in Ironton, Ohio, where visiting priests from the Most Precious Blood Provincial House awakened in him a call to the priesthood. He entered the Society's novitiate in 1917, going on to St. Joseph College in Renselaer, Indiana, St. Charles Seminary in Carthagena, Ohio, and ordination on February 21, 1929, in the Carthagena Seminary chapel. By 1933 he had obtained a licentiate in Sacred Theology and a Ph.D. from the Catholic University of America where he taught for a year.

Bishop Joseph M. Marling C.PP.S. ordains Father John W. Buchanan to the Holy Priesthood on April 6, 1957, in the Cathedral of St. Peter in Jefferson City. Fr. Buchanan was the first priest to be ordained in the new diocese.

In 1939 he was the youngest general provincial ever elected for the U.S. province established in 1844. As provincial, he oversaw the updating of the Society's Constitutions and began a mission in Latin America.

In 1946 he was appointed auxiliary bishop of Kansas City by Pope Pius XII and ordained on August 6, 1947. He became a highly sought after speaker, retreat master and spiritual director, attracting hundreds to his Sunday afternoon classes for adults.

Appointed to head the new diocese of Jefferson City in 1956, Bishop Marling was installed by Archbishop Joseph E. Ritter of St. Louis in November at the Cathedral of St. Peter in Jefferson City.

During his tenure in Jefferson City, Bishop Marling built the new Cathedral plus 25 churches, 29 schools, 30 rectories and 16 convents besides providing a new Carmelite monastery. He cultivated priestly and religious vocations, inviting priests and sisters from out of the diocese, including Ireland. The establishment of St. Thomas More Newman Center in Columbia and the diocesan newspaper, The Catholic Missourian, are also among his innovations. He also established St. Thomas Aquinas boarding high school seminary in Hannibal.

Bishop Marling participated in all four sessions of Vatican II. In implementing its decrees, he focused on liturgical and ecumenical reforms and creation of the Priests Senate, Parish Councils, Sisters Association and Priests' Study Weeks.

In response to Pope John XXIII's call for priests in South America, he opened the diocese's Peru Missions, which he visited three times a year.

Scholar, creative innovator, skilled negotiator, voracious reader, outstanding preacher and holy, dedicated order priest, after his retirement in 1969, Bishop Marling traveled, wrote and lectured even as he helped out as associate in Christ the King parish, Kansas City.

Shortly after his golden anniversary as priest, Bishop Marling succumbed to cancer and died at age 75 on October 2, 1979, in Kansas City. He was a bishop for 32 years.

Bishop Michael F. McAuliffe (left) second bishop of Jefferson City; and Bishop Joseph M. Marling C.PP.S., founding bishop, at a celebration for Bishop Marling's 50th priestly anniversary, concelebrated in the Cathedral of St. Joseph in Jefferson City on April 25, 1979.

PART TWO: A VIBRANT NEW DIOCESE (1956-1984)

A ltogether, within 20 years an almost complete spiritual revolution in the Church of the Heartland took place. Bishop McAuliffe's far-seeing policies of the 1970s regarding the importance of religious education of all, especially of adults, bore fruit. Catholic schools, CCD and adult religious education were all geared toward formation in the spiritual life. Bishop McAuliffe set up a separate Office of Education to provide training for the changes called for by Vatican II.

☙ *Bishop Michael F. McAuliffe poses with Pope Paul VI in the Vatican during Bishop McAuliffe's 1972 ad limina visit.*

The Carmelite nuns were invited in 1960 to give witness to the importance of contemplative prayer. A House of Prayer was opened in Sedalia as an experiment and a Renewal Center was set up in Moberly. Other movements centered on spiritual development were Cursillo, Marriage Encounter, Teens Encounter Christ, Quest, Natural Family Planning, retreats, missions and days of recollection.

The aim of "Agenda: Renewal" was to provide the services of a caring and nurturing Church for every area of life. It constituted both a support system for those services as well as a means of awareness of needs. Emphasis was placed on the training of lay ministers and women religious as pastoral ministers. Young adults were encouraged to give a year of service to their Church.

Thus the Diocese of Jefferson City, with its lower Catholic population and lack of prestige and wealth capitalized on its ability to afford its members personal contact, give shining witness to its growth in faith and excel in its social concerns, especially in its missions in Peru, its concern for the role of women and, containing more prisons than any other state, its charitable outreach to prisoners. As it constitutes the exact physical center of the United States, it strove to be the heart of the nation—a place where people developed sensitivity to the needs of others and stood out in its concern for the land and its resources.

THE CATHOLIC CHURCH EXTENSION SOCIETY

F ATHER Francis Clement Kelley established the Catholic Church Extension Society in 1905 in Chicago. Moved by the poverty he saw in rural and remote America, Fr. Kelley started Catholic Extension to extend the resources of the Church so that Catholics in these areas could practice their faith and receive the sacraments like their brothers and sisters in larger cities. Many of these areas or "missions" were so remote that Catholic Extension used railroad chapel cars or "chapels on wheels" to reach them. Catholic Extension's work always has been funded entirely by generous donations from caring Catholics and is carried out with zeal by thousands of priests, religious and lay missionaries.

By the mid-20th century, the society was issuing grants to dioceses in rural parts of the country to help pay for churches, schools and rectories. Catholic Extension support has helped build more than 10,000 churches in the United States. Many parishes in the Jefferson City Diocese owe the existence of their simple, solid parish buildings to Catholic Extension grants.

HE was born on November 22, 1920, in Kansas City, Kansas, the second of the six sons of John Joseph McAuliffe and Bridget Agnes (Broderick) McAuliffe. He was baptized on December 12, 1920 at St. Benedict Church in Kansas City, Kansas.

The Bishop attended Our Lady of Good Counsel Grade School, Kansas City; St. John High School Seminary, Kansas City; St. Louis Preparatory Seminary; and Catholic University of America, Washington, D.C.

He was ordained a priest at the Cathedral of the Immaculate Conception, Kansas City on May 31, 1945, and celebrated his first Mass at Our Lady of Good Counsel Church, Kansas City on June 3, 1945. His first assignments were at St. Canera, Neosho, and as Auxiliary Chaplain to Camp Crowder. Archbishop O'Hara encouraged him to pursue graduate studies in Washington, DC in 1948, where he earned a Doctorate in Sacred Theology in 1954.

Bishop Michael F. McAuliffe following his ordination as a Bishop in 1969

John Joseph Cardinal Carberry of St. Louis at the Cathedral dedication in 1974

Upon his return to Missouri, he was an associate pastor, a high school instructor and counselor and director of education before becoming pastor of St. Therese, Kansas City from 1959-1967 and founding pastor of St. John Francis Regis, Kansas City from 1967-1969. In 1957 he was named Papal Chamberlain and promoted to Domestic Prelate in 1961.

Bishop McAuliffe served on the diocesan Tribunal in 1948 and 1953. He was Director of the Confraternity of Christian Doctrine and simultaneously diocesan Director of Religious Vocations before becoming Diocesan Superintendent of Schools from 1957-1967. He was Secretary of Education and Vicar of Religious Education in 1967. He was a Diocesan Consultor twice and sat on the Diocesan School Board; the Seminary Board; the Commission on Sacred Liturgy, Music and Art; the Catholic Reporter Advisory Board; the Committee on Doctrinal Instruction; and on the Diocesan Preparatory Commission for the Synod. At the time of his appointment as bishop, he was in his second term as a member of the Kansas City Human Relations Commission, having been appointed by Mayor Ilus W. Davis.

Upon the resignation of Bishop Joseph M. Marling, Pope Paul VI appointed him the Second Bishop of Jefferson City on July 2, 1969. He was ordained and installed on August 18, 1969 at the Cathedral of St. Joseph in Jefferson City. His motto, "In Truth and Charity," reflects the ideals of St. Francis de Sales, his baptismal patron.

The new bishop strengthened and promoted the Catholic School Office by creating the Diocesan Religious Education Office, the Directions 80 program, in 1983 "Our Journey in Faith," and the Diocesan Excellence in Education program, which assisted Catholic teachers' salaries in 1995. Bishop McAuliffe also established the following ministries: Permanent Diaconate Office, Ministry to Priests, Social Concerns, Spiritual Renewal of the Laity, Family Life, Youth Ministry, Charismatic Renewal, Communications Office, Campus Ministry, Marriage Encounter, Cursillo, Teens Encounter Christ, and Residents Encounter Christ.

While Bishop McAuliffe dedicated 21 new churches during his years as bishop, his greatest joy was to witness the dedication of the Cathedral of St. Joseph during the centennial of the death of Father Ferdinand Helias, S.J., the Apostle of Central Missouri.

The bishop began the Diocesan Fund Appeal in 1972 and the Diocesan Pastoral Council in 1973. During his tenure, he ordained 78 priests and 84 permanent deacons. He ordained the first group of permanent deacons at the Cathedral in 1977.

Bishop Michael F. McAuliffe distributes Holy Communion during an outdoor Mass in Peru.

Nationally, the Bishop was active in the United States Conference of Catholic Bishops and in the Missouri Catholic Conference. He was Episcopal Moderator of the National Catholic Committee on Scouting from 1970-1979, and Chairman of the Bishops' Committee on Women in the Church from 1974 – 1982. Bishop McAuliffe also served on various other USCCB committees including the Administrative Committee, Committee on Missions, Committee on Latin America and Committee on Vocations.

On the local level, Bishop McAuliffe was on the Conception Seminary Board of Regents, the Missouri Christian Leadership Forum, the Missouri Catholic Conference and the Board of Trustees of Kenrick-Glennon Seminary. He also chaired the Coalition Against the Death Penalty.

In the civil arena, the Bishop was the Grand Prior of the Knights of the Holy Sepulchre, Honorary State Chaplain of the Missouri Knights of Columbus six times and a member of the Cathedral Council, Jefferson City.

At the time of his death in 2006, Bishop McAuliffe had been a priest for 60 years and a Bishop for 36 years.

Holy Family window at St. Joseph, Salisbury

The
Young Ladies Sodality

THREE:

Be Not Afraid 1984-2006

Pope John Paul II offered Mass for about 350,000 on a farm in rural Iowa during his first pastoral visit to the United States in 1979, bringing to international attention the vigor of Catholicism in the heart of America's breadbasket.

For Catholics in central and northeastern Missouri, the decade that followed brought new opportunities for growth and evangelization.

In 1980, Bishop McAuliffe launched the Directions 80 initiative to work with the entire diocese to cultivate lay leadership in parishes and ensure that the Church's changing needs would continue to be met in the future. Out of that initiative flowed the fruitful diocese-wide spiritual renewal program, "Our Journey in Faith." -- a three-year process of prayer, discussion, activity and liturgical celebration specifically aimed at encouraging spiritual renewal and building up lay leadership.

The community marked its silver jubilee in 1982. Archbishop John L. May of St. Louis presided at Mass in the Cathedral of St. Joseph on April 23. Joining him at the altar were not only Bishop McAuliffe and priests of the diocese, but also Father John R. Gaydos, the master of ceremonies who would become Bishop McAuliffe's successor 15 years later.

1983 brought the first major revision of the Code of Canon Law since 1917, and with it came more responsibility for the diocesan curia. Many judicial matters previously handled at the Vatican were placed under the

Jesus with little children

jurisdiction of diocesan bishops. The staff of the diocesan tribunal grew.

The diocese purchased two houses on Clark Avenue next to the main Chancery building to accommodate additional staff as the diocese renewed its commitment to Catholic education and outreach, youth ministry, the missions and resettlement. Also, renovations to the Chancery building made more space for diocesan staff after the Missouri Catholic Conference moved to the building across the street.

The diocese joined the rest of the Church in observing the 1950th anniversary of the death and resurrection of Christ, from March 25, 1983, through Easter Sunday 1984.

Following the ordination of the first group of permanent deacons in the diocese in 1977, the number and diversity of diaconal ministries continued to grow.

Catholics simultaneously continued praying for more priests to serve their spiritual needs, while coming to appreciate the previously underestimated value of leadership from religious sisters and laypeople. Several parishes hired pastoral ministers and pastoral administrators to help a shrinking number of priests carry the burden of running parishes and reaching out to people with ever-diversifying needs.

Sister Mary Margaret Johanning SSND became the first woman to serve as diocesan chancellor. Religious sisters would follow her into that position after she lost her fight with cancer.

Churchwide ecumenical efforts following the Second Vatican Council were trickling down to the most rudimentary spheres of ministry, with Catholics in parishes throughout the diocese joining forces with Christians from other churches to help people in need, improve their communities, and advocate for better public policy.

Priests, religious and laypeople throughout the diocese heeded Pope John Paul's warnings against a pending culture of death. Local Catholics took leading roles in protecting pre-born children through direct advocacy, policy initiatives and material support for mothers in unplanned pregnancies.

Some of the loudest voices against the reinstitution of capital punishment in Missouri came from the heartland. More than 100 people stood in the rain and prayed outside the old Missouri State Penitentiary in Jefferson City at midnight as the first death sentence in years was carried out there in 1989.

The diocesan Refugee and Immigration Services had been handling waves of immigrants, beginning mostly with Vietnamese, Laotian and Cambodian refugees following the Vietnam War; then Iranians following the

᷍ *Stained-glass window portraying the Holy Cross in St. Anthony, St. Anthony.*

Iranian Revolution; then Central Americans during political unrest; then refugees from Central Europe; then the Congo and the Sudan. For years, parishes throughout the diocese would "adopt" these immigrants and help them assimilate into the American culture. More recently, many of these immigrants have had assistance settling in more heavily populated areas in the diocese, where they are able to maintain kinship among people from their own countries while becoming Americans.

As demographics in the state continued to shift, hospitality continued to emerge as a hallmark of the diocese.

Tourist and recreation industries near the Lake of the Ozarks, Truman Lake and Mark Twain Lake continued to attract Catholics from throughout the state and country. An increasing number of Catholic legislators converged in Jefferson City during legislative sessions, as did Catholics who moved to the Capital City to work in state government.

Until the completion of several new maximum-security prisons statewide, the diocese was home to as much as 80 percent of the state's prison population. Catholics in parishes throughout the diocese established and cultivated a strong presence in each correctional institution, allowing Catholics there to continue practicing their faith.

Catholic outreach on college campuses in the diocese continued to expand in depth and scope, with the parishes in Kirksville, Rolla and Jefferson City supporting Newman Centers on nearby campuses, and a growing college contingent at St. Thomas More Newman

᷍ *Cardinal John J. Carberry of St. Louis visits with Pope John Paul II in Rome 1988. With them is Monsignor (later Bishop) John R. Gaydos, who was serving as chancellor of the St. Louis archdiocese.*

Center parish in Columbia. Increased participation in Sunday Masses and weekday activities at those centers would eventually lead to new or expanded facilities in Columbia, Kirksville and Rolla.

With new waves of immigration from Central and South America, mostly from Mexico, the diocese began working with parishes to provide material and spiritual support for their new Spanish-speaking members.

Lay movements in the Church — including Cursillo, Marriage Encounter, Residents Encounter Christ (for prison residents), and Teens Encounter Christ — continued to cultivate the life of the Church, one weekend at a time.

In solidarity, the faithful of the diocese weathered the farm crises of the 1980s and 90s, ranging from bad economic policy to droughts to the Flood of 1993. At the same time, new industries were emerging that would change the economies of many communities in the diocese. Food processing plants in places such as Milan, California and Sedalia would attract immigrants from Mexico and other Spanish-speaking countries. Several parishes began offering Masses in Spanish and fine-tuning their efforts toward helping people in need.

Priests from the diocese continued working with other priests, consecrated religious and lay Catholic missionaries in giant Catholic parishes in Peru to provide not only for the spiritual needs of their congregants but also the basic material needs of all Peruvians. Catholics in central and northeastern Missouri proved themselves to be among the most generous in the United States in supporting the diocese's Peru missions.

Bishop McAuliffe retired after 28 years as bishop in August 1997, and Pope John Paul II sent Monsignor John R. Gaydos, former vicar general of the St. Louis archdiocese, to succeed him. Archbishop Justin F. Rigali of St. Louis ordained the new bishop to the episcopacy. Bishop Gaydos resolved to lead the diocese "with a shepherd's care."

Bishop John R. Gaydos meets with Pope John Paul II during Bishop Gaydos' Ad Limina visit in July 1998.

As Pope John Paul II continued calling the entire Church to commit itself to a new evangelization at the dawn of Christianity's third millennium, Bishop Gaydos announced the beginning of a Pentecost experience for the Jefferson City diocese: Disciples in Mission. The three-year experience, built around diocesan, parish and small-group prayer and worship, helped Catholics fall more deeply in love with Scripture and see themselves as true evangelizers among acquaintances and in the world.

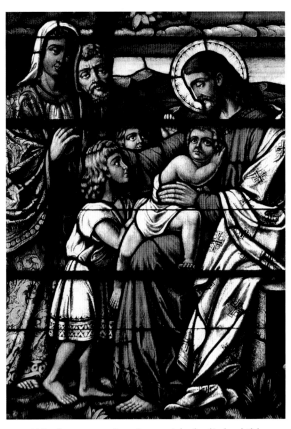

Window portraying Jesus with the little children at St. Thomas the Apostle, St. Thomas

The Pope returned to the heartland in 1999, with hundreds of people from the Jefferson City diocese attending the Papal Youth Gathering and the Papal Mass in St. Louis.

That same year, in anticipation of Disciples in Mission, a specially built cross containing a relic of the True Cross began a "pilgrimage of reconciliation" from parish to parish to encourage fervent prayer for the success of the three-year experience through the merits of Christ's passion, death and resurrection.

The Church's great Jubilee 2000 celebrations focused on Christ fully present in the Eucharist, and culminated with a two-day diocesan Eucharistic congress in Columbia. Thousands attended the catechetical sessions. The following afternoon, priests of the diocese joined Bishops Gaydos and McAuliffe at the Altar from the Pope's historic 1999 visit to Missouri for the largest Mass in the diocese's history. About 3,000 Catholics converged in the Hearnes Center sports arena on the campus of the University of Missouri for this Eucharistic celebration.

"What a beautiful sight you are, the face of Christ in the heart of Missouri!" the bishop exclaimed.

Diocese of Jefferson City
50th Anniversary
1956 – 2006
Proclaiming the Good News : Memory and Mission

֍ *Diocesan jubilee prayer card.*

Parishioners heeded the Disciples in Mission call for recommitment to being evangelizers, proclaimers of Christ; people of life, prayer, conversion, faithfulness, mission and especially the Eucharist.

On that foundation, the bishop in 2001 formulated his Pentecost vision for carrying out Christ's mission in the diocese. Likening the new-millennium Church to the Apostles in the Upper Room awaiting a commission from Christ to evangelize all people, he recommitted himself and the Diocese of Jefferson City to five specific aspects of Christ's mission: Evangelization; sacramental unity; lifelong spiritual education and formation; helping the needy, weak and suffering; and unity of worship.

That same year, Americans looked bewilderedly into the face of international terrorism as the towers of the World Trade Center fell, and soldiers were sent overseas to fight the War on Terror.

Following Disciples in Mission and suitable discernment, Bishop Gaydos convened a new Diocesan Pastoral Council -- made up of clergy and lay and consecrated religious members -- to advise him on matters of evangelization and pastoral planning. The DPC is made up of representatives of the eight deanery councils, which are comprised of representatives of each parish.

The new century has seen an increase in devotional practice in the Church. Pope John Paul II proclaimed a Year of the Rosary in 2003, hoping to cultivate a richer awareness of this powerful devotion. At a diocesan Rosary celebration, at Immaculate Conception in Loose Creek, Bishop Gaydos noted how many people he had seen throughout the diocese praying the rosary daily.

When Pope John Paul began a Year of the Eucharist in October 2004, Catholics in central and northeastern Missouri joined the rest of the Universal Church in returning to parish-based Adoration of the Most Blessed Sacrament. Several parishes in the diocese had been holding round-the-clock adoration for years; others began holding regular adoration.

֍ *Pope Benedict XVI receives Bishop John R. Gaydos on October 5, 2005, outside St. Peter's Basilica.*

🔊 *The new Alphonse J. Schwartze Memorial Catholic Center, with its illuminated, cross-topped lantern above the main entrance, is an impressive landmark, especially at night.*

🔊 *Emil Schwartz, chairman of the Alphonse J. Schwartze Community Foundation, and Bishop John R. Gaydos break ground in April 2004 for a new Catholic Center to be named in honor of the late Alphonse Schwartze, who was Emil's brother. The foundation, administered by Mr. Schwartze's family, paid for the center as a token of appreciation for all God had done for and through Mr. Schwartze, a lifelong Westphalia parishioner, in his 95-year life. It was the largest single gift in the diocese's 50-year history.*

The death of Pope John Paul II sent waves of grief throughout the world. He was the only Pope an entire generation of Catholics had known. The Universal Church united in prayer as Christ's long-suffering vicar was laid to rest, and did so again with joy a few weeks later as his successor, Pope Benedict XVI, was elevated to the papacy.

The Alphonse J. Schwartze Community Foundation, established by a prominent lifelong Westphalia parishioner and recipient of papal honors, in 2003 offered to build a new Catholic Center to replace the scattered and tired chancery offices on Clark Avenue. Diocesan employees moved into the new Alphonse J. Schwartze Memorial Catholic Center, on the grounds of the Cathedral of St. Joseph, in July 2005.

The Jefferson City diocese's Golden Jubilee celebration began that same summer. Coinciding with the Year of the Eucharist, the kickoff celebrations included Masses, Eucharistic processions and other acts of devotion.

Echoing the fervent daily prayers of the diocese's founding bishop — who had taken Mary as his middle name and had consecrated the diocese to the Immaculate Heart of Mary — Bishop Gaydos chose for the official diocesan jubilee prayer the "Memorare." Attributed to St. Bernard of Clairvaux, the prayer connects the past 50 years of handiwork to the intercession of Christ's Mother, and calls upon her for continued help in the future:

"Remember, O most gracious Virgin Mary that never was it known that anyone who fled to thy protection, implored thy help or sought they intercession was left unaided. Inspired by this confidence, I fly unto thee, O Virgin of Virgins, my mother. To thee I come, before thee I stand, sinful and sorrowful. O Mother of the Word Incarnate, despise not my petitions, but in thy mercy hear and answer them. Amen."

🔊 *More than 3,000 Catholics from throughout the Jefferson City diocese gather in the Hearnes Center in Columbia on August 20, 2000, for a Mass to close the diocesan Eucharistic Congress. It was the largest Mass in the diocese's history.*

Latin Papal Document establishing new Dioceses in Missouri by Pope Pius XII in 1956.

John Raymond was the first-born son of George J. Gaydos and Carrie Lee (Pearson) Gaydos. He was baptized at their parish church, St. Agnes, in South St. Louis. He was born in St. Louis, Missouri on August 14, 1943.

EARLY EDUCATION

Bishop Gaydos' education began at his parish school in 1948, continued at St. Louis Preparatory Seminary in 1957 and Cardinal Glennon College in St. Louis in 1961. In 1965, he was sent to Rome to study at the Pontifical Gregorian University. He was ordained for the Archdiocese of St. Louis by Bishop Francis F. Reh, rector of the Pontifical North American College in St. Peter Basilica, Vatican City, on December 20, 1968.

The following year he completed his studies and returned to the States to be assigned as associate pastor of St. Joseph Parish, Manchester, Missouri. From 1974 to 1977 he ministered as associate pastor of St. Cecilia, St. Louis, until in 1977 he became secretary to the Archbishop and Master of Ceremonies at liturgical functions. He held that position for thirteen years, serving Cardinal John J. Carberry and then Archbishop John L. May.

Archbishop John L. May of St. Louis sprinkles concelebrating bishops with holy water at the beginning of a Mass in the Cathedral of St. Joseph to celebrate the diocese's 25th anniversary in 1982. Serving as the archbishop's master of ceremonies (in cassock and surplice, near center of photo) is Father John R. Gaydos of St. Louis, who would become Jefferson City's third bishop in 1997

After serving as pastor of St. Gerard Majella, Kirkwood, Missouri, from 1990-1996, Monsignor Gaydos was appointed Vicar General of the Archdiocese of St. Louis in 1996. The next year, on June 15, 1997, he was appointed Bishop of Jefferson City by Pope John Paul II and was ordained and installed as third Bishop of Jefferson City on August 27, 1997, by Archbishop Justin F. Rigali of St. Louis.

PART-TIME ASSIGNMENTS

As a priest of the Archdiocese of St. Louis, Bishop Gaydos held a number of special part-time assignments. Four years after becoming a priest, he held positions on the faculty of St. Louis Preparatory Seminary, South (1972-1977), the Archdiocesan Committee of the Permanent Diaconate (1975-1982), Priests' Council (1976-1979), Committee for the Permanent Diaconate as secretary (1977-1980) and editor of the archdiocesan Yearbook (1977-1987).

Just nine years after his priestly ordination in 1977, he was appointed Assistant Chancellor of the diocese, secretary to the Cardinal and Secretary of Seminaries. In 1981 he was named Chancellor of the Archdiocese. Five years later, in 1986, Pope John Paul II named him an honorary prelate and in 1990, he became Knight Commander of the Holy Sepulcher.

EPISCOPAL ENGAGEMENTS

As the third bishop of Jefferson City, Bishop Gaydos has ordained seven men to the priesthood, 21 to the permanent diaconate and signed thousands with the oil of chrism in the sacrament of confirmation.

As episcopal leader, he uses his gifts by sitting on committees that influence the direction of the local and national church. He was a member of the NCCB Committee on Priestly Life and Ministry from 1997-2003, serving as the chairman from 2000-2003. As a committee chairman, he served on the USCCB Administrative Committee from 2000-2003. He was a member of the National Retired Religious Organizations Advisory Committee (1998-2001). His zeal for evangelization led him to become a member of the National Council of Catholic Bishops (NCCB) Committee on World Missions (1998-2000). Earlier editorial positions lent him experience to work as a member of the NCCB Committee on Communications (1999-2002). Since 2000 he has been a member of the USCCB Ad Hoc Committee on Sex Abuse.

Bishop John R. Gaydos at his installation in the Cathedral of St. Joseph in 1997

The bishop's lifelong interest in education has found an outlet in membership of the Conception Seminary Board of Regents since 1997 and the Board of Governors of the North American College from 1998 to 2001 and from 2003 to the present.

After the terrorist attacks in New York and Washington in 2001, Bishop Gaydos joined his voice with fellow bishops of Missouri to issue a statement noting that instead of tearing apart the human family, as the perpetrators hoped, the tragedies of that day brought people from all the world closer together through acts of heroic sacrifice, compassion and prayer. The statement dealt with the problem of evil and suggested further appropriate responses to the event. Among them was honest reflection on American culture and the US international social and economic policies underlying divisions in the Middle East. The bishops ended with an admonition to all to promote a culture of life and a civilization of love.

Crucifixion window at Visitation Church, Vicuna

FOUR:

Parishes of the Diocese of Jefferson City

Resurrection window at Holy Guardian Angels, Brinktown

Cathedral of St. Joseph, Jefferson City
1959

The Cathedral Church of Saint Joseph is the embodiment of the vision of the first Bishop of Jefferson City, Bishop Joseph M. Marling, CPPS, following the Second Vatican Council. The parish and school had their beginnings earlier on April 6, 1958, when Bishop Marling announced the formation of a new third parish on the west end of Jefferson City. Monsignor Joseph A. Vogelweid, P.A., the first Vicar General of the Diocese, selected St. Joseph as the patron.

On a 19-acre site on West Main Street, the construction of the buildings began that same year. The first red brick building, three stories tall, housed a cafeteria in the basement, the temporary church on the first floor, and six classrooms on the second floor. Fr. Kenneth J. McDonnell, serving during construction, was the first pastor. The new parish had 250 original families.

The church-school cost approximately $275,000. The rectory was constructed next at approximately $275,000, and a convent was built in 1960 for approximately $40,000. The convent was to house the Sisters of Mercy who had been recruited from Ireland by the second pastor, Msgr. Francis O'Duignan, who served until 1964. The first Mass was celebrated in the new church-school on September 25, 1959.

Monsignor Gerard L. Poelker was installed September 10, 1964, as the third pastor and first rector. It was during his tenure in 1966 that plans were made to build a modern, circular Cathedral. On August 20, 1967, Bishop Marling presided over a groundbreaking

ceremony. Prost Builders was selected to construct the new church at a cost of $1.2 million. It became the Cathedral and the entire diocese assisted financially and spiritually.

When the first Mass was celebrated by Bishop Marling on December 25, 1968, the parish had 650 households. Fr. Kenneth J. Brockel was the first diocesan priest ordained in the new cathedral on May 24, 1969. Bishop Michael F. McAuliffe was ordained and installed here on August 18, 1969. The Reverend Richard Cronin was installed as Administrator in June 1970.

In 1973 Fr. Francis G. Gillgannon succeeded Fr. Richard Cronin as administrator until 1982. A change in bishops delayed the formal dedication of the Cathedral until May 5, 1974, when John Joseph Cardinal Carberry, Archbishop of St. Louis, presided over the formal blessing. When Bishop Marling died on October 2, 1979, he was buried from the cathedral.

The school was growing and changing. The original school on the upper floor of the church had only six rooms for grades 1-6. With the completion of the cathedral, the original church-school facility was remodeled into classrooms. In 1977, an activities building was constructed to house a gym with a stage. Since overcrowding was a problem, in the early 1980's after Reverend Patrick J. Shortt was assigned as rector

Cathedral of St. Joseph, Jefferson City, front view

09 *Archbishop John L. May of St. Louis sprinkles concelebrating priests with holy water at the beginning of a Mass in the Cathedral of St. Joseph in Jefferson City to celebrate the Jefferson City diocese's 25th anniversary in 1982. Serving as the archbishop's master of ceremonies (in cassock and surplice, near center of photo) is Father John R. Gaydos of St. Louis, who would become Jefferson City's third bishop.*

09 *Interior of the Cathedral*

in 1982, planning began on an addition to the school, completed in 1984, which connected the activities building with the school. Classrooms were also constructed in the basement of the convent. On September 25, 1984, Bishop McAuliffe celebrated the Silver Jubilee of the parish. Perpetual Adoration began in 1986.

The school administration was changed from the Sisters of Mercy to a secular principal in 1987. By 1989 the school was staffed totally by laity. The convent was then converted into parish offices on the upper two floors, with classrooms remaining in the basement for the first grade and later for the kindergarten. The rectory became a private home.

Fr. Michael J. Wilbers was named rector in June 1989. He also served as the third Vicar General. Under his leadership the cathedral parish became debt free. The Silver Jubilee of the first Mass in the cathedral was marked on December 25, 1993, by Bishop McAuliffe, who retired in 1997 and resided in the parish.

On August 27, 1997, the Most Reverend John R. Gaydos was ordained and installed as the third Bishop of Jefferson City. The Most Reverend Justin F. Rigali, Archbishop of St. Louis, served as consecrator.

The Cathedral parish is currently planning for future expansion. Bishop Gaydos broke ground for the new Chancery Office on April 1, 2004. The Alphonse J. Schwarze Memorial Catholic Center was completed and occupied on July 26, 2005.

The parish serves 4,200 parishioners in 1,397 households. The school has an enrollment of 474 with 26 teachers.

The Knights of Columbus Council was established here in 2001; it has 275 members. Five priests and four sisters have come from the parish to serve the Church.

09 *Door decoration featuring Christ as Lord of the Universe and Teacher Supreme*

St. Peter, Jefferson City
1846

ᘒ *Interior of the church*

ᘒ *Sanctuary of St. Peter, the first Cathedral.*

The first St. Peter Church was erected in 1846 from the forest wilderness that comprised Jefferson City. It stood on the site of what is now St. Peter School. The present church was built in 1881, dedicated on August 12, 1883 and was placed on the National Register of Historic Places in 1976.
It is across the street from the State Capitol.
Until 1968 St. Peter served as the first Cathedral.

ᘒ *St. Peter, Jefferson City*

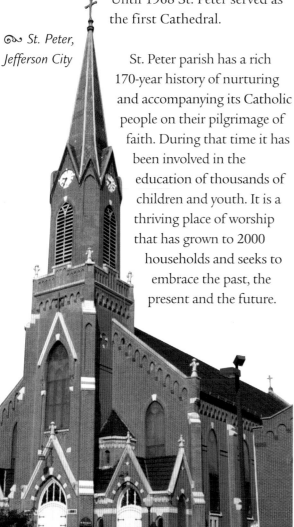

St. Peter parish has a rich 170-year history of nurturing and accompanying its Catholic people on their pilgrimage of faith. During that time it has been involved in the education of thousands of children and youth. It is a thriving place of worship that has grown to 2000 households and seeks to embrace the past, the present and the future.

ᘒ *Stained-glass window of the Baptism of Jesus*

Immaculate Conception, Jefferson City
1913

Jefferson City's second parish, Immaculate Conception, was established in 1913 by Rev. John B. Pleus. Its 110 families hailed from the east end of the city. Within a year a rectory and school were built.

The present Romanesque church was dedicated on May 30, 1923 by Archbishop John Glennon.

Two strengths of the parish are evident.

It is one of the largest parishes in the diocese and thus has the luxury of many talented parishioners to help in its mission. The parish council and commissions are very active, providing a rich source of expertise and energy.

Immaculate Conception School currently enrolls more than 500 students.

᳇ *Statue of Christ of the Highway on the church grounds*

᳇ *Immaculate Conception, Jefferson City*

᳇ *Stained-glass window of the Nativity*

᳇ *Classic lines of the sanctuary with round stained-glass windows*

St. Aloysius, Argyle
1910

Before the Rock Island Railroad came through Osage County and the town of Argyle came into existence, Catholic settlers in the area were served by the St. Boniface Parish in Koeltztown.

St. Aloysius, the patron saint of young people, was chosen as the name for the new church, which was completed in 1910. Fr. Jeseph Rapien was its first pastor.

Fr. Joseph Clooney, who served in Argyle from 1919 through 1925, decided that the church should be built in the form of a cross. To accomplish this the building was cut in two and the sacristy was pulled back 25 feet by John Curtis of Vienna, Mo. Curtis moved buildings with horses and a track and pulley system. The cross addition was then built to fill in the gap, extending the church's width by about six feet on each side.

Church interior

Longtime Argyle resident Joe Brunnert recalls that parishioners built scaffolding from oak trees such that branches and green leaves extended into the church for a time. During the construction phase, to receive Holy Communion, parishioners had to walk on planks spanning the divide between the church and the sacristy.

The building was remodeled in the 1960s according to the Vatican II dictates, and again in 1985 and 2005.

St. Aloysius, Argyle, dedicated July 11, 1910

St. Boniface, Koeltztown
1866

Koeltztown is named for a Protestant, Miss Eremline Koeltze, who purchased large tracts of land south of Westphalia. To attract German Catholics, she donated 10 acres and building funds for a Catholic church and cemetery to the Most Rev. Peter Kenrick, Archbishop of St. Louis.

A log church was completed in 1861 with Fr. John Goelding offering the first Mass. Before that, Fr. Helias, a Jesuit priest, would ride by mule into the area to celebrate Mass at the Hermann Sandbothe home.

The parish grew and construction of the current brick church began on June 5, 1877. The old log church was converted into a school. A new rectory was built in 1891 and a new school completed in 1910. The School Sisters of Notre Dame took over direction of the parochial section of the building, which was shared with public school students until 1913. On June 8, 1951, the church steeple was severely damaged in a windstorm, but rebuilt in 1952.

ᖇ *St. Boniface, Koeltztown; Mission of St. Aloysius, Argyle, dedicated June 5, 1910*

St. Boniface parish contributed to the building of parishes in Folk, Freeburg, Meta, and, most significantly, Argyle. Almost half of St. Boniface members began attending St. Aloysius when it opened in 1910.

ᖇ *Interior, St. Boniface*

ᖇ *Stations of the Cross*

St. Alexander, Belle
1908

Until the end of the last century, there were many Catholic families in Belle and the surrounding countryside. Their parents were German and Irish immigrants strong in faith. Lacking a near-by place to worship, some of these families eventually joined one of the local churches, but others held onto their faith by crossing the fields and Gasconade River into Rich Fountain every Sunday for Mass. Prominent among these were the Baumgartners, Klebbas, Meitzler, Nies and Sieglers.

In 1841, John Reed donated two acres of his property in Cleavesville to the bishop of St. Louis, and that year a new church under the patronage of St. Michael, was built on the site. At first the Jesuit Fathers of Washington, Missouri, administered the church. Later priests from Owensville, Westphalia and Rich Fountain administered it irregularly. The last Mass was offered there in 1909.

Dr. Joseph Tellman, who moved to Belle in 1904, arranged to have priests coming sporadically to offer Mass in his new home. In 1908, he was able to buy a suitable site for a Catholic church within the town. By June of 1910, with the generous support of other local families, the doctor succeeded in building a new log church dedicated to St. Alexandeer that was to serve for the next 60 years

At first the new church was a mission of the Owensville parish with Fr. Julian Moczydlowski and successive pastors coming once a month by train to offer Mass and instruct the children.

&ldots; *Interior of St. Alexander*

When the road between Belle and Owensville was constructed in the 1920's, some Catholics were able to attend Mass weekly by traveling to Owensville. In 1947, Mass became available weekly all year.

With the erection of Jefferson City to the rank of diocese in 1956, Belle became the responsibility of the pastors from Linn until 1972 when the pastor of Chamois assumed that role. By that time, the parish had grown to 80 families. A second Mass was added every weekend and work was begun on a new brick church.

At present the parish has 50 active families. Monthly breakfast at St. Alexander has become a Belle tradition. The addition of a parish center afforded additional classrooms to Belle Elementary School for several years. St Alexander's continues to provide a vital link to the Belle community.

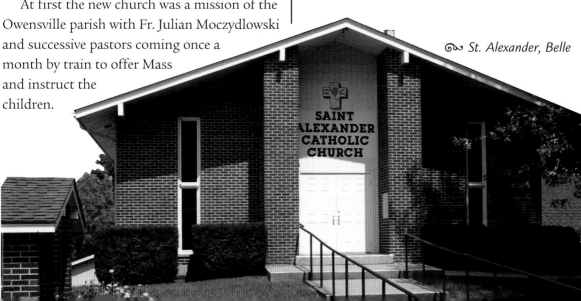

&ldots; *St. Alexander, Belle*

St. Aloysius, Baring
1894

ᔕ *Marian Grotto Shrine*

ᔕ *Shrine to St. Aloysius, parish patron*

ᔕ *St. Aloysius, Baring*

In the late 1800's, the post-Civil War westward expansion carried a host of Catholics who found a home in Baring, a thriving railroad community. As it flourished, the need for a Catholic Church became obvious.

On July 10, 1893 Archbishop Peter Kenrick, the Archbishop of St. Louis, acquired the land and with the help of the Catholic Church Extension Society, St. Aloysius Church was built. On November 13, 1893, Bishop John J. Kain dedicated the new church, St. Aloysius Gonzaga.

In 1922, the church was expanded to a seating capacity of 450. In 1926, a brick veneer was added to the exterior of the church, along with stained-glass windows.

The parish hall was constructed in 1940. In 1955, the Grotto of the Immaculate Conception was built from porous rock that was gathered from around New London.

Parishioners also added decorative rocks they had gathered or had on hand. In 1972 a new rectory was built to replace the old one. For 123 years the community of St. Aloysius has taken great pride in their church and their mission of sharing Christ's presence in northeast Missouri.

Shifting demographics in the late 1900's caused parish numbers to dwindle, and in 2004 St. Aloysius was closed for weekend Masses. This has been a painful experience for the people, but it did not indicate the end of the Catholic community. They still gather together as a parish community to celebrate life, death and resurrection. They are committed to continuing their parish identity while at the same time, sharing parish life with the people of St. Joseph Church in Edina.

St. Louis of France, Bonnots Mill
1905

One of the most beautiful locations for a temple of the Most High is that of Bonnot's Mill in Osage County. Bonnots Mill is the oldest town in Osage County. Original settlers, mainly early French fur traders, established French Village, which stood very near the present Bonnots Mill. Jesuit Fr. Ferdinand Helias arrived in the area in 1838 and was the first priest to minister to the Catholics in French Village.

St. Louis of France Parish was established in 1905. Archbishop John Glennon of St. Louis purchased three acres of land for the parish for $6. The property covers the entire bluff above the Missouri Pacific Railroad tracks and overlooks the confluence of the Osage and Missouri rivers. When St. Louis church was completed, Msgr. Otto Hoog, V. G., dedicated it on July 17, 1906.

Fr. Charles Even was named the first pastor of the new parish. He served from 1905 to November 1922. He is buried in the St. Louis of France cemetery, the only one facing the town he loved.

The parish school opened in 1916. It was staffed by the Sisters of Divine Providence in 1932, the Ursuline Nuns in 1943, and once again the Divine Providence sisters in 1950, who remained until the school closed in 1966.

A parish hall was added to the complex in 1954.

Parishioners who serve in religious life include Fr. George Kramer and Sisters of Divine Providence Ferdinand Marie (Catherine) Meyer, deceased; Bernadette (Georgia Ann) Meyer; and Cecilia (Irma) Jansen. Sr. M. Stella (Iona) Kane, deceased, became a Sister of Mary.

ﬡ *St. Louis, Bonnots Mill*

ﬡ *The Crucifixion memorialized outdoors*

SS. Peter and Paul, Boonville

ᘐ *Interior of Ss. Peter and Paul*

In 1838 Fr. Ferdinand Helias, S.J., celebrated Mass in the Anthony Fox, John Foy and Hilden homes. Records indicated that the first church was built in 1851, others say 1856. The first school was built and cemetery property was purchased in 1856.

In 1857 Fr. John Hogan (later Bishop) intended to celebrate Mass on the Feast of the Assumption, but could not because the pastor, who was gone on a mission, took the only chalice and vestments available.

Between 1869 and 1875 the first parish rectory was built. Within the next 10 years, the school was enlarged and a transept, sanctuary and sacristies were added to the church. On March 2, 1890, the nave was badly damaged by fire. A new section with a tower and side turrets was added and dedicated on November 16, 1890.

An unusual feature of the parish school is that one of its teachers,

ᘐ *SS. Peter & Paul, Boonville*

Fr. Francis E. Hagendorn, later became the first chancellor of the newly created Diocese of Jefferson City. A new school and convent were built in 1925 and a new parish rectory, in 1954.

SS. Peter and Paul was chosen as the host parish for the first organizational meeting called by Bishop Joseph M. Marling to establish the diocese on October 16, 1956.

In June 1972, groundbreaking ceremonies were held for a colonial style church, completed in August 1973 and dedicated on September 23, 1973, by Bishop Michael F. McAuliffe. A new parish office building was built in 2001 with new pews and carpet installed in July 2004.

In 1978, the parish rejoiced when Fr. Lawrence J. McNamara, a former associate pastor, was ordained Bishop of Grand Island, Nebraska. SS. Peter and Paul has sponsored Vietnamese and Cambodian families. Parish organizations include Parish Council, School Board, PTA, CYO, Knights of Columbus, Ladies Auxiliary, Daughters of Isabella, Living Rosary and the Legion of Mary. The parish has six religious vocations and three permanent deacons.

St. Francis, Bourbon
1915

In 1910 Bourbon had 10 Catholic families who decided to build a church. The church of St. Francis Carracciolo was dedicated on June 14, 1914. The church has as its patron the 16th century Italian priest who was co-founder of a religious congregation to combine the active and the contemplative life.

For many years St. Francis was on the circuit of priests who served Rolla.

At the present it is served by the priest at Cuba.

From the 1930's to the 1970's, St. Francis was served by a number of pastors and pastoral administrators. On October 15, 1983 a new multipurpose building was dedicated on Old Highway 66. It serves as both the church and the parish center.

୬୦ *St. Francis, Bourbon*

Holy Guardian Angels, Brinktown

1891

Prior to the Civil War, German immigrants John Wolfgang Viessman, born a Lutheran, and his wife Teresa Lauterbach settled in western Maries County founding a small town known as Viessman Station. For several years Mass was held in the Viessman home where a bureau served as the altar.

In 1874, the couple donated four acres to Archbishop Peter Richard Kenrick for a church and cemetery. Viessman and his neighbors built the church, known as Holy Trinity, of logs. The building was later used as a Catholic school until it burned in 1904.

A new wood-frame church was erected 1891-92 and by 1903 the settlement was renamed Brinktown. By this time, the parish was known by its present name: Guardian Angels. In 1956, a brick church replaced the wooden one and served the Brinktown community until it was destroyed by fire on April 15, 1996.

Under the leadership of Fr. John Schimtz, the church was rebuilt and dedicated in November 22, 1998. For many years, the Guardian Angels Fall Supper has coincided with a trail ride that ends at the church.

Guardian Angel stained-glass window

Holy Guardian Angels, Brinktown

Immaculate Conception, Brookfield
1859

Immaculate Conception parish had its beginning on December 20, 1859, the year the town was incorporated. Rev. J.J. Hogan, the first pastor, found many Irish Catholic settlers employed by the railroad hungering for spiritual nourishment through the sacraments. Fr. Hogan would go on to become bishop of St. Joseph and then of Kansas City, Missouri.

Fr. J. J. Hogan, first pastor

In its 145 years of existence, under the guidance and efforts of 17 pastors and several religious communities serving as educators, a strong community of faith flourished. Presently the parish serves 240 households. Members are from 10 towns and surrounding rural areas.

The parish mission is to spread the kingdom of Jesus Christ everywhere so that all may be brought into relationship with him and share in his saving redemption. It serves and is served in this mission by:

First church built in 1860

Camp Caritas summer Bible school students and staff celebrating its 25th anniversary in 2004.

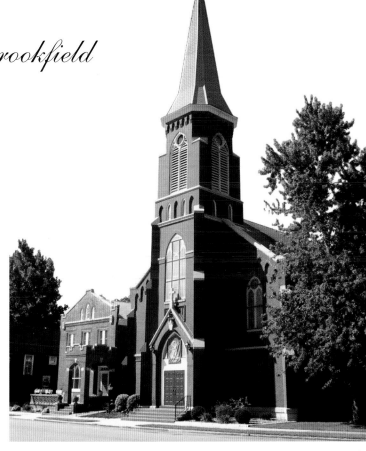

Immaculate Conception Church and Rectory, Brookfield

Sanctuary of Immaculate Conception

- nurturing the faith of its members
- working for the unity of all people
- reaching out to evangelize the unchurched
- ministering to the social needs of the immediate environment and
- developing a care and concern for the world Church.

We undertake this mission in the spirit of love and dedication to patterning our lives ever more faithfully on the Gospel.

Saint Boniface, Brunswick
1860

Catholic families were among the early settlers of Brunswick. Services were held in various homes until 1860 when Fr. John Hogan began the first parish in Brunswick by renting the old City Hall. Later a frame church was built on a hill overlooking the surrounding territory. The parish was placed in the charge of the Franciscan Fathers.

By 1901 the frame church was too small and lots were purchased to the south of the church site. Ground was broken for the 90-by 37-foot pressed brick and stone structure that continues to serve the parish today. It was dedicated on October 26, 1902 by Bishop Maurice Burke of St. Joseph.

In 1939 the interior of the church was destroyed by fire, the cause of which could not be determined because every part of the church was damaged.

In the late 1980s, Fr. Judge oversaw extensive remodeling of the church and rectory. The school building, which, together with the rectory had been erected in 1925, was razed and a parking lot was constructed in its place.

Thirty-nine priests have served the parish community since its inception 145 years ago.

❧ *Gothic altar under an arched ceiling, St. Boniface*

❧ *St. Boniface, Brunswick*

Saint Raphael, Indian Grove
1886

The Catholic congregation of St. Raphael was started by pioneers from Ireland, Germany, Switzerland and other countries. Since there was no church, Mass was celebrated in the home of Anastasia Senn. On August 25, 1885, the foundation for a new church was laid and dedication took place on June 2, 1886 by Bishop Hogan. At the time, the priest would stay the weekend and hold instructions for initiates.

In July 1914 the parish was placed under the direction of the Franciscans, but later it was returned to diocesan priests. On December 15, 1955, Fr. Lawrence Speichinger, the first native of the parish to be ordained, offered his first Mass. On September 8, 1974, Sr. Mary Raphael Speichinger, the first woman of the parish to enter religious life returned to celebrate her jubilee with Fr. Lawrence.

Although the parish remains small, fourth and fifth generations of the original families continue in active service to parish life. All through the years, the church and cemetery have been well cared for. On June 9, 1996, at 11 a.m., with the church bell tolling 100 times, the parish celebrated its 110th anniversary.

St. Raphael, mission of St. Boniface, and cemetery set in the rural countryside of Indian Grove

St. Joseph, Hurricane Branch
1877

The history of St. Joseph, Hurricane Branch, shows that as early as 1858 Catholic families of the surrounding counties gathered once a month in private homes to attend Mass celebrated by Fr. John Hogan, then pastor at Chillicothe. Fr. Hogan continued his missionary work for more than 20 years. When Pope Pius IX appointed him bishop in 1878, the new bishop ordered the construction of St. Joseph Church.

The project was carried out by the Franciscan Fathers of St. Mary of the Angels at Wien, who continued to care for the parish until 1914.

When the town of Marceline was founded in 1888, Bishop Hogan immediately established a new parish in honor of the Franciscan Cardinal, St. Bonaventure. Since 1925 St. Joseph and St. Bonaventure have shared parish priests. Both the Parish council and St. Anne Altar Society are active in the parish. At the present time, the church is undergoing redecoration.

❧ *Statue of patron St. Joseph*

❧ *St. Joseph, Hurricane Branch*

Annunciation, California
1872

Annunciation window

Circular sanctuary with wood furnishings

Annunciation Parish traces its origins to the missionary efforts of Fr. Ferdinand Helias, S.J., in 1857. With the building of the Missouri Pacific Railroad, many Irish families settled near California, and together with a few German families, a congregation was formed.

A parish school was established in 1889. This building, along with the church, was destroyed by fire in 1900. Both were rebuilt, but the second school burned in 1982 and was not rebuilt. A new church was dedicated on June 23, 1985.

Annunciation, California

Recent years have seen growth in the Hispanic population in California and the surrounding area. Annunciation tries to meet their needs as it strives to incorporate them into the parish.

Assumption church in Cedron, built in 1838 and closed in 1993 has also been part of Annunciation parish.

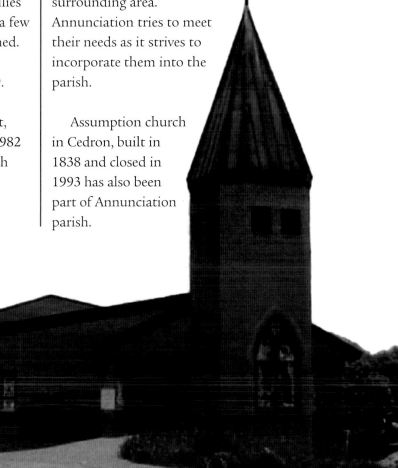

St. Anthony, Camdenton

St. Anthony, Camdenton
1946

From its humble beginnings in 1947 when the first Mass was celebrated in a private home by the then pastor of Sacred Heart Church, Eldon, to the present Eucharistic celebrations in the beautiful, new church dedicated by Bishop John R. Gaydos on June 13, 2000, the parish community has been noted for its participation in the faith life of the parish and its active community outreach.

The first church building was an army Chapel purchased from Camp Crowder, Neosho, Missouri, in 1948. After being moved to its new location to serve the small community, it was dedicated by Bishop Joseph M. Marling, Auxiliary Bishop of Kansas City, on May 30, 1948. As the community and tourism grew around the Lake of the Ozarks, a new church was built on the same location in the early 1970s. Its membership expanded to nearly 100 families. A new rectory, completed in April 1979, was destroyed by fire on December 1, 1987. During this period, as many as five Masses were offered on each weekend to accommodate the large crowds of visitors. In 1989 Reiters Motel, located next to the church property, was purchased, its rooms converted to classrooms and a church office. In 1993 a new rectory was purchased some five miles from the church.

As tourism and the community continued to increase in the 1990s, it became apparent

First Church in Camp Crowder

that further expansion was necessary. At this time about 75 acres became available on the north side of Camdenton, three miles from the church. On it were constructed first, a new Education Center providing 13 classrooms, and then a new church with a new parish office was dedicated on November 19, 2000. The rectory was added in 2002.

St. Anthony is a vibrant, faith-filled community, which continues to grow in community activities and spirituality.

Confirmation at St. Anthony

It serves approximately 600 resident families plus weekenders and many visitors during the summer months and holiday seasons. Our Lady of the Snows, Climax Springs, is its mission church.

Spirit-dominated sanctuary

Our Lady of the Snows, Climax Springs
1990

Our Lady of the Snows Mission Church was established in January 1983 as an outdoor Mass station under the guidance of Fr. Joseph Starman on land donated by Fred & Louise Baker. The initial planning meeting was held at Baker's Resort and was well attended.

In 1987 through the generosity of our local community a permanent church was built on land donated by Noland Helm using volunteer help.

A boat dock was built to provide pick-up service for people across the lake. Our Lady of the Snows is a friendly little church in the woods.

↬ *Father Joseph Starmann, founder of the Mission of Our Lady of the Snows in Climax Springs, poses near the altar following an outdoor Mass in August 1984 with Pat and Charles Brown, George and Libby Hermelink and Lyle and Terry Bartels. Aug. 17, 1984.*

Wood-paneled sanctuary, window lit

St. Joseph, Canton
1895

The first priest to celebrate Mass in Canton rode horseback from Edina. The first Catholic church building was erected in 1841 at a town called Tully (evacuated in 1851) near Canton not far from the site of today's Lock and Dam No. 20 on the Mississippi River. The bricks from that church were used to construct St. Joseph Church in 1869. The present church was dedicated on October 30, 1954 by Bishop John Cody.

St. Joseph had a Catholic school from 1904 until 1916. The current rectory and hall was erected in 1976 during Fr. Stephen Sandknop's pastorate and completed before his untimely death at the age of 38 in June 1976. A parish hall was added in 1981 during Fr. Gerald Kaimann's pastorate.

The parish, which is composed of approximately 110 households, has an active parish council, a Ladies an Altar Sodality, a CCD program and a weekly Scripture study group. Over the years the parish has taken an active part in the Canton Council of Churches. Many parishioners have also participated in various renewal programs such as Cursillo, Marriage Encounter, TEC, and QUEST.

Statue of Jesus at the Pillar

The St. Ann Altar Sodality annually sponsors a soup supper in February. The parish council annually sponsors a Septemberfest.

St. Joseph, Canton and Marquette Hall

Notre Dame, La Grange
1868

The history of Notre Dame LaGrange parish dates from 1865 when land for the first church building was purchased. The new Immaculate Conception Church was blessed in 1867. The parish, which consists today of approximately 45 active households, has always been a mission parish of St. Joseph in Canton. For a few months in 1893, the parish was thought to have dissolved from lack of parishioners and the church building sold, only to be deeded back and the parish re-established. In the 1920s Mass was discontinued and the Catholics of La Grange rode the train to Canton for Mass.

A new church building was erected during the pastorate of Fr. Michael J. O'Rourke and completed in 1949. It was given the title of Notre Dame Church. This church building was damaged by flooding of the Mississippi River in 1973. A new, multipurpose church building and hall was constructed on higher ground in 1983, dedicated on August 19, 1984, and serves the parish well today.

Notre Dame Parish, consisting of approximately 44 households, has an active parish council, a St. Mary's Altar Society, and a CCD program. The Altar Society spearheads parish social functions and sponsors a Spring

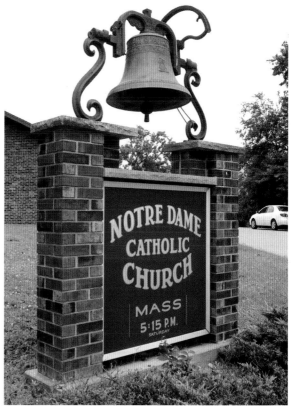

ᡦ *The bell calling parishioners to worship at St. Joseph*

Brunch and Fall Bazaar. Being a mission parish from St. Joseph Parish in Canton, 7-1/2 miles away, the same priests and pastoral administrators who have served Notre Dame parish have also served St. Joseph parish.

ᡦ *Notre Dame, La Grange; Mission of St. Joseph, Canton*

Holy Spirit, Centralia
1897

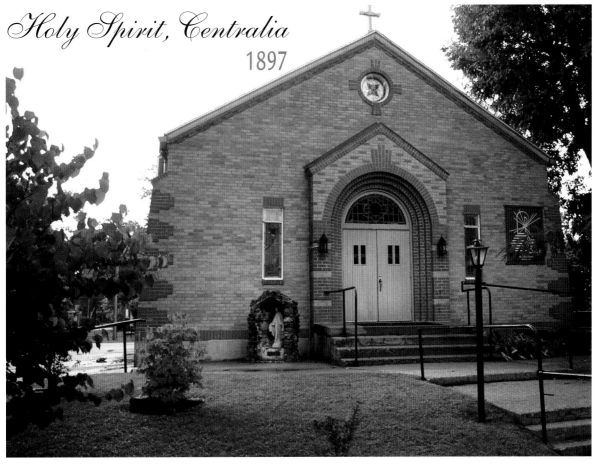

🖜 *Holy Spirit, Centralia, with shrine was dedicated on July 4, 1947.*

Catholics of Centralia were first served in 1859 by Fr. John J. Hogan who was to become the first bishop of St. Joseph and later of Kansas City. One of the "Prairie Queen Missions," Holy Ghost (now Holy Spirit) was attended by priests of surrounding towns.

By 1869, three years after the parish's establishment, a Catholic church was built at Sturgeon, which then closed, although parishioners worshipped at Centralia or Moberly until 1949. A wood-frame church erected through the generosity of a donor, opened in Centralia in 1904.

The windows of the present church, built by the pastor and parishioners in 1941 for $16,000, tell the gospel stories. From 1942 to 1945 the parish operated a school. Until the arrival of Mill Hill Missionaries from Britain, the parish was attended by diocesan priests.

🖜 *Interior of Holy Spirit*

In 1987 a multi-purpose building was constructed. In 1996 parishioners built a new altar and pulpit, and, outdoors, a grotto to Our Lady that rests on stones from Sturgeon.

Holy Spirit offered the first priest to the new Diocese of Jefferson City in 1957, Father John W. Buchanan.

Most Pure Heart of Mary, Chamois

1865

❧ *Most Pure Heart of Mary with belfry, Chamois*

Most Pure Heart of Mary parish was formed in 1865 in Chamois. Long before the town was established, as early as 1838, Jesuit Fr. Ferdinand Helias visited the area. A former store building served as the first Catholic church in Chamois and was blessed in 1871. From 1875 to 1908 the parish had no resident priest and was attended by the Franciscan fathers from Hermann, Missouri. A new church was dedicated on May 30, 1912, and was remodeled in 1980.

❧ *Camp Hope 2004*

❧ *May Crowning May 2, 2004: (l-r) Brady Stone, Karina Mehmert, Brent Dudenhoeffer, Jacob Keilholz, Lucas Skaggs*

❧ *Turtle Races at the parish picnic*

St. Patrick, Clarence
1884

Soon after Clarence was incorporated in 1866, Catholic families of German and Irish descent opened businesses under names of Langenbach, Riley, Hogan, Hunolt, and Cleary. Some accounts maintain that Bishop Hogan had said Mass in the area as early as 1855. Father Cahill from Macon celebrated Mass in the homes.

The first St. Patrick Church was dedicated March 17, 1884. The first resident pastor was Father John F. Kenny, and St. Michael's at Hagers Grove became a mission of St. Patrick.

In 1960, Father Willam Ludwig and the people of St. Patrick built a new church and rectory, dedicated on May 7, 1961.

The centennial of St. Patrick Church was celebrated March 17, 1984, with Bishop Michael McAuliffe celebrating the Mass. Msgr. John C. Mahoney, the last resident priest, came in 1976, and St. Patrick was consolidated with St. Mary's in Shelbina. At his first Mass at St. Patrick's, Father Mahoney said, "If God will just give me four more years, there is no end to what we can accomplish." He continued to say this every four years until his death in 1991. Today, St. Patrick's continues to be a spiritual force in the Clarence community, and the parish's St. Patrick's Day Dinner is famous throughout Shelby County and beyond.

❧ *St. Patrick, Clarence*

Our Lady of Lourdes, Columbia
1958

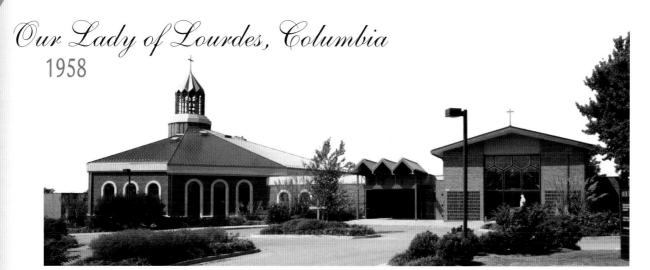

🐚 *Our Lady of Lourdes, the largest parish in the Diocese of Jefferson City*

🐚 *Dedication by Bishop Marling in 1958*

🐚 *Majestic sanctuary in the round*

Our Lady of Lourdes traces its roots to 1831 when the first Masses were celebrated by circuit-riding priests from Boonville, Glasgow and Mexico, Missouri.

From 1881 to 1958 the spiritual needs of the Catholic community were provided for by Sacred Heart, the first permanent parish in Columbia. Conceived by the Archdiocese of St. Louis in 1956, Our Lady Of Lourdes was established as part of the newly formed Diocese of Jefferson City. Bishop Joseph Marling formally dedicated the original church on October 19, 1958.

In 1999 a new church was built at the same site to accommodate the growing parish. Bishop John Gaydos dedicated it on October 17, 1999. The building project included an educational center in the basement of the new church and the renovation of the original worship space to be used as a parish hall.

🐚 *Young parishioners participate with Bishop John Gaydos in the groundbreaking for the new church.*

Sacred Heart Church, Columbia
1876

Catholic services were first attended in the homes of pioneers in Columbia in 1835. In 1881 worship was held monthly in the new frame church with a 75-foot spire. The present limestone Romanesque church was dedicated November 8, 1914 by Archbishop Glennon.

Through the years, the parishioners of Sacred Heart generously contributed to the Knights of Columbus "Student Home Building" erected in 1920, the Sacred Heart School in 1927, the Sacred Heart Activity Building in 1951, the Newman Center and Our Lady of Lourdes Parish and Columbia Catholic School. In 1969, the Sacred Heart School closed.

In 1947, there were five masses in the church and one in the activity building each Sunday. Sacred Heart gave more than 100 years of special

ministries to the university and college students of Columbia. Today Sacred Heart's history and tradition continues to draw new parishioners from 38 countries.

Sacred Heart is celebrated nationally for its choir, which strives to give its best efforts to the Lord and its parish community each week.

⌘ *Sanctuary lighted by three round, stained-glass windows*

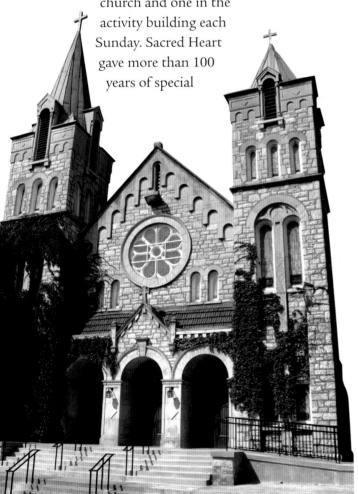

⌘ *Sacred Heart, first parish in Columbia*

⌘ *Baptismal and Holy Water Font at church entrance*

St. Thomas More Newman Center, Columbia
1963

S t. Thomas More Newman Center was established as a parish in 1963. A church was built on a prime location adjacent to the University of Missouri in 1964. The campus ministry mission was coupled with that of a parish from the beginning. In 1994 the addition of a new worship space and the renovation of old space into classrooms continued the mission of serving the community of resident parish families and thousands of college students. The Sunday 9 p.m. Mass is popular with collegians

൭ *The Baptismal Pool for full immersion*

൭ *Close up of altar and sanctuary*

൭ *St. Thomas More, Columbia*

൭ *College students display musical talents in their annual fundraiser for charity*

St. Cornelius, Crocker
1966

ᐷ *Church interior*

ᐷ *The sanctuary of St. Cornelius Church in Crocker, shortly after its completion in 1966.*

St. Cornelius parish was organized in 1962. On October 29, 1962, Fr. Peter Walsh celebrated Mass in the local funeral home chapel.

Later seven acres of land on the north edge of town were purchased.

Upon its completion and furnishing, the church was dedicated by Bishop Marling on April 3, 1966.

ᐷ *St. Cornelius, Crocker*

Holy Cross, Cuba
1880

The first Holy Cross Catholic Church was erected in Cuba in 1880. In 1924 the first permanent pastor, Fr. Curtis J. Hornsey, purchased the Haskell Manor and 10 adjoining acres. The Manor became the convent of the School Sisters of Notre Dame and the first Catholic elementary school between Pacific and Springfield in 1928.

In 1936/1937 the current fieldstone church was built. The stone was gathered from miles around for the outside walls, fence and altar. In 1940 the present rectory was also built of fieldstone just east of the church, and in 1952 the new rock Holy Cross School and Parish Hall were built. The latest addition to Holy Cross School was completed in 2004 with four new spacious, bright classrooms and a large entry foyer. The exterior rock architecture was maintained. The parish hall was also remodeled with the addition of a new state-of-the-art kitchen.

The exterior of Holy Cross parish buildings has been acclaimed by many as one of the finest examples of native stone architecture in Missouri. Only flint stone was used because, unlike sandstone, it weathers brightly. Bishop Gaydos rededicated the school and renovation of St. Nicholas Hall in October 2004.

ᖇ᠉ *The interior of Holy Cross Church was remodeled in 2004*

ᖇ᠉ *The bell tolls from Holy Cross Church throughout the city of Cuba*

ᖇ᠉ *The addition to Holy Cross School/St. Nicholas Hall was completed in 2004*

St. Theresa, Dixon
1928

Although the church honoring St. Theresa of Lisieux was built in 1925, it was not to become an established parish until 1928. If not the first church to be named in honor of St. Theresa (canonized May 17, 1925), it very well may have been among the first in the world.

On August 8, 2004, Bishop John Gaydos, together with visiting priests, parishioners and former parishioners, celebrated the 75th anniversary of the parish.

St. Theresa serves the natives of an area of breathtaking beauty. Others who have moved in, along with both active and retired military also form the congregation.

The parish motto and goal is summed up in the words: "We are Family."

◈ *Smiling Madonna in a Holy Family at the Nativity stained-glass window*

◈ *Sanctuary showing brickwork*

◈ *St. Theresa, Dixon, dedicated on June 21, 1970*

St. Joseph, Edina
1844

St. Joseph parish traces its roots back to the pioneer settlement days of Edina. As early as 1837 Roman Catholic frontiersmen commenced to settle in Knox County. The first Mass offered in the county was in June 1843 in a log house. As more Catholics arrived, a log church was completed in 1844. In 1857, to accommodate German and Irish immigrants, determined to build a lasting community in the wilderness, the brick church was erected. In 1864 the present rectory was built. Westward expansion necessitated an even larger church. In 1873, ground was broken for the present church with a 195-foot spire. In 1885, a pipe organ from the US Centennial, the largest west of the Mississippi, at that time was installed.

The Sisters of Loretto established a school in 1895. Their residence was dedicated in 1902. The high school served the area for 55 years until its closing in 1954. The grade school continued to flourish until 1996 when it closed after 130 years of service.

🙟 *Sanctuary with baldachino over the altar*

🙟 *St. Joseph, Edina dedicated on October 10, 1875*

St. Joseph is more than just brick and mortar. It is a community of believers who for 160 plus years have passed on their legacy of faith and witness to the abiding presence of Christ in northeast Missouri. St. Joseph has interpreted and reacted to the signs of the times. Expanding their outreach, in 2002 a diocesan retreat center was opened in the old convent building. Their legacy of faith has produced many religious vocations and fostered a strong commitment to youth and adult religious formation.

Time may have taken its toll on the economic security of the area, but time has also served to strengthen the faith, hope and love of this community.

LAID BY
RT. REV. P. J. RYAN
JULY 5. 1874

🙟 *Cornerstone of church*

66

The original church in Eldon, built in 1910, still functions as part of Lee House, a large retirement center.

A confirmation class before the altar of the old church in Eldon built in 1910.

The wood-paneled sanctuary

Side-chapel

Sacred Heart Church of Eldon is in Miller County. However, the foundations for this parish were laid to the west in Morgan County. In 1863, ten Irish Catholic families settled in Morgan County. By 1868 they had started to build a stone church on what is now state road "O," just east of Laurie. This was the beginning of the Catholic presence in the area.

Some Catholic families settled in Eldon prior to 1900, happy to have a priest come occasionally (usually from Morgan County) to celebrate Mass in one of the Catholic homes. By 1910 the congregation was able to build a church in Eldon on the corner of North Mill and North Streets.

Carved Holy Water Font

In 1929 the Union Electric Company began the construction of the Bagnell Dam. This brought in many more Catholics to work on the project. Growth of the town and the parish made it necessary to build a larger church in 1961 at 540 North Mill Street. The growth of tourism at the Lake of the Ozarks has caused the parish to grow to the 355 households it lists today, welcoming many more vacationers and tourists through its doors each Sunday.

Sacred Heart, Eldon with triple-bell tower dedicated November 5, 1961

Queen of Peace, Ewing
1887

ᢓᢧ *Queen of Peace, Ewing, dedicated on October 12, 1958*

Queen of Peace parish in Ewing, Lewis County originated as far back as 1868 when visiting priests would occasionally celebrate the Mass and the sacraments.

However, the official beginning of the parish was in 1887 in a caboose, and the centennial of the parish was celebrated in 1987. The first parishioners were of German, Irish and French origin. In the past the parish has been known as St. Mary and Immaculate Conception. The name Queen of Peace was adopted in 1919 when the second church building was dedicated. The present, third church building dates from 1958. During its history the parish has been a part of three dioceses—St. Louis until 1911, St. Joseph from 1911-1956, and Jefferson City since 1956. From 1898 to 1918 the parish had a parochial school called St. Mary, which was the first free parochial school in the Archdiocese of St. Louis.

The parish has the distinction of having been served briefly by the first full-blooded Negro priest in the United States, Fr. Augustine Tolton. He sang the Mass at the laying of the church cornerstone on May 31, 1889, and ministered there in later years.

The parish, which has approximately 120 households, has an active parish council, a ladies sodality, a quilting group, a CCD program and a Knights of Columbus Council. A new and spacious parish hall was erected and dedicated in 2002 during Fr. David Cox's pastorate. The parish sponsors a summer picnic in July and a spaghetti dinner in February, as well as other social events as needed.

ᢓᢧ *Carved-wood altar with reredos and wood-paneled walls and ceiling*

Sanctuary

St. Joseph, Fayette
1956

St. Joseph parish was organized in 1879 by Fr. Anton Pauck as a mission of St. Mary's parish in Glasgow. The first church building was blessed November 5, 1890. St. Joseph's became a parish in 1900 with Fr. Joseph Kroeger as first pastor. St. Joseph returned to mission status in 1908 and was placed with Sacred Heart parish in New Franklin. Because of a very small congregation, St. Joseph's was closed sometime after 1920.

In 1954 Joseph Cardinal Ritter, Archbishop of St. Louis, expressed a desire for a new church in Howard County, and Fr. Thomas Sullivan was appointed pastor. Groundbreaking for the new St. Joseph's took place in Fayette just after Easter 1956. The cornerstone for the L-shaped structure was laid May 30, 1956. The first Mass was Midnight Mass at Christmas 1956, dedication on March 19, 1957.

St. Joseph's had a resident pastor until 1978 when Father McDonnell retired. St. Joseph's again shared a priest with either SS. Peter and Paul in Boonville or St. Mary in Glasgow. A team ministry of sisters was established in 1979 to work in the parish. In the early 1980's, Sister Dorothy Miller was appointed as the first resident pastoral administrator of the parish, while the priest continued to travel from either Boonville or Glasgow. The parish continued to grow to about 120 families plus the Catholic college students from Central Methodist College in Fayette.

In 1980, discussion was started about the construction of an education/activities building.

After much planning, work began on the 60' x 100' building on July 28, 1992. The building, completed by March 1993, has eight divided classrooms, a kitchen, restrooms, and storage area.

St. Joseph's regained a resident pastor in 1996. In the fall of 2001, work was begun on new stained-glass windows for the church. St. Joseph found itself without a resident pastor again in 2002 as Fr. Robert Duesdieker from SS. Peter and Paul in Boonville was assigned to serve the parish. The mortgage on the education/activities building was paid off in 2002. Work continues on the stained-glass window project and on building up the life of the parish community.

St. Joseph, Fayette

St. Anthony of Padua, Folk

1905

St. Anthony of Padua parish was founded in 1905 on the faith of 47 families who wanted a place to worship that was nearer their homes. Monsignor Otto Hoog of the Archdiocese of St. Louis, granted them permission to form the parish of St. Anthony of Padua in Folk, Missouri, and assigned Rev. John Hoeschen as the first pastor. The first Mass was celebrated on Pentecost Sunday, June 11 1905.

In 1948 construction began on the current church structure under the direction of Rev. Raymond Willerding. Today 85 families of St. Anthony of Padua Parish celebrate the centennial of the parish on June 11, 2005, with Bishop Gaydos. St. Anthony shares a priest with Westphalia.

  St. Anthony of Padua, Folk

Our Lady Help of Christians, Frankenstein

Our Lady Help of Christians Church was organized in 1863. The church had three different locations in its first 27 years: on a wood knoll, in a valley and on a high ridge. German and Irish immigrants settled at Frankenstein where a parish was started and named Mary, Help of Christians. The German name, Maria Hilf was in use for many years. The origin of the name Frankenstein is disputed. Some say the town was named for Gottfried Franken who donated part of the land. Others say the town was named for a benefactor in Germany named Frankenstein.

The building of the present church of Romanesque design was launched in September 1922 and dedicated on September 1, 1923. The exterior and the bell tower are of quarried native limestone. Thousands of cubic yards of stone were blasted out of a quarry about a mile away and hauled up a long hill by means of team and wagon. A mule was used to lift the stones into place. The roof is of red Italian tile. Parishioners donated most of the labor. The church stands today as a living memorial to the priests and people of Frankenstein who built it with love and sacrifice as a gift to God.

The school saw various sites as well. In December 1962 it was decided to replace the 1909 structure with a new school, which was staffed by the School Sisters of St. Francis until 1980. Generations of church members have received their education there.

Our Lady Help of Christians has a consistent membership of about 150 families. Because it is a small, rural parish, it has kept a family image with the people assuming responsibility for carrying out the parish's ministry and giving generously of their time and talents in the building and upkeep of the parish property.

◌ *Interior of the church*

◌ *Our Lady Help of Christians, Frankenstein*

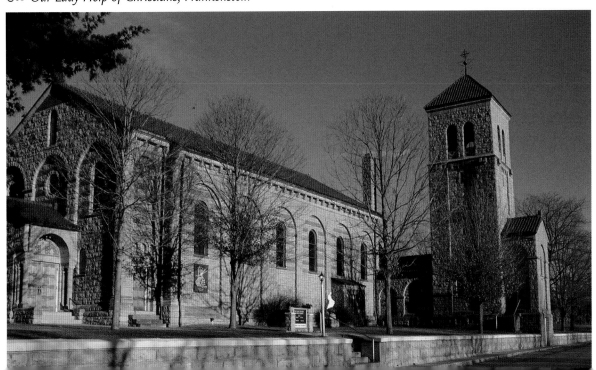

Holy Family, Freeburg
1904

Holy Family parish, Freeburg was founded in 1904. As a small wooden chapel, the church stood directly to the west of the present church. Not many years later, it was discovered that the church would be too small for those attending services.

In the spring of 1920, ground was broken and the foundation built of solid rock began for the present church, which today is known as the "Cathedral of the Ozark" for its Romanesque architecture design and twin 96-foot steeples with gilded crosses pointed towards heaven, raising heart and mind to God. It was dedicated on August 8, 1921.

Holy Family Church, measuring 127 by 45 feet, is built in the form of a cross. The transept measures 66 feet, clearly showing the cross form. The inside height from floor to ceiling is 40 feet. As soon as the new church was plastered, pews were put in place enabling the people to attend Mass before construction was complete.

ᘒ *Sanctuary and side altars*

In 1920, it was the last Missouri church built in European style. Five large windows on each side measure 21 feet; the others 17 feet in height. The present windows in Romanesque style were installed in 1952. They hold picturesque designs of the Vineyard of the Vine and the branches from St. John's Gospel 15:1-8. The window over the choir is the "God the Father" (the creating, sustaining hand of God). The east window is the "God the Son" (Lamb of God) and the west window is the "Holy Spirit".

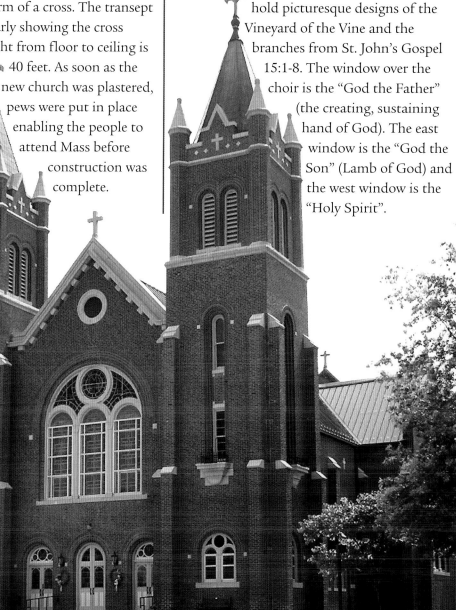

ᘒ *Holy Family, Freeburg*

72

St. Peters   Sun-Gazette

❧ *A picture of the exterior of the first St. Peter Church*

The establishment of the Catholic Church's presence in Callaway County began in 1831 when the Jesuit priests built two missions, one of which was in Fulton, Missouri. St. Peter Church was built in 1875 on Nicholas Street and was served for 30 years by priests from neighboring towns. The church was erected as a parish with its first resident pastor in 1905. St. Peter School opened in 1934. In 1956, the school and parish were moved to new buildings at the current location on corner of State Road Z and Wood Street and in 1990 an additional four classrooms, a kitchen and multipurpose building were added. Precious Blood Sisters from O'Fallon, Missouri (1934-69), Irish Sisters of Mercy (1969-76) and the Sisters of Christian Charity from Wilmette, Illinois (1992-present) have all taught in the school and served the parish under the guidance 23 diocesan priests as pastors.

This small parish encompasses the communities of Auxvasse, Calwood, Hatton, Kingdom City, Millersburg, New Bloomfield and Williamsburg, as well as Fulton. The parish includes five high schools: Missouri School for the Deaf, Westminster College, William Woods University, State Mental Institutions & Penitentiaries. It also has two hospitals, a nuclear power plant and the Winston Churchill Memorial - site of the "Iron Curtain" speech.

Historically and today, St. Peter parish strives to be a Catholic presence in a non-Catholic county. In the early- to mid-20th century, its now senior parishioners were shunned from business and social activities because they were known to be Catholic. In this new millennium, St. Peter parishioners struggle to better model Catholic identity in a secular world. Nonetheless, the Catholic presence is known and felt by the Fulton community in its witness to the faith, its quality of education to its students, its social concerns outreach, and the commitment to Catholic values and morality.

❧ *Sr. Mercedes Johnson, S.C.C enjoys a Senior Social afternoon.*

❧ *Sanctuary*

❧ *St. Peter, Fulton with shrine and bell dedicated April 7, 1957*

St. Mary, Glasgow
1866

St. Mary parish on the bluffs of the Missouri River was established in 1866 after an influx of Catholic Irish and German immigrants to the region. Fr. Henry Meurs, the founding pastor, directed the construction of the first church and school.

The original church, completed in 1869, was built on the site of the present school and was replaced in 1913 by the church that stands today. On a visit to the parish in 1909, prior to the completion of the new church, John Cardinal Glennon, Archbishop of St. Louis, stood on the hill and pointed to the distant bluffs saying, "The day is not too far distant when a modern passenger steamer will round yonder bend and an enthusiastic passenger will point out to his expectant fellow travelers a speck in the sky with the word, 'There's Glasgow; I see the cross on St. Mary's Church.'"

In the 1890s a large, antebellum home, which had been occupied by Union troops during the Battle of Glasgow in the Civil War, was purchased by the parish as the new rectory. Construction of the current school building was completed in 1919. The present parish was carved out of the original St. Mary parish, Immaculate Conception parish from nearby Aholt in the old St. Joseph Diocese and All Saints Catholic Church in West Glasgow, the outer boundary of the old Kansas City Diocese. The three parishes were combined in the 1950s when the present Diocese of Jefferson City was established.

Since its founding, St. Mary parish has remained a very close-knit rural parish and continues to play a vital role in the life of this historic community.

St. Mary's first rectory, built about 1875 during the pastorate of Fr. Ernest Zechenter.

Procession in front of the rectory during the Civil War.

St. Mary, Glasgow, dedicated on May 11, 1913

Holy Family, Hannibal

❧ *Interior at Holy Family Church*

❧ *Holy Family Church welcomes a new member to the church through the Rite of Christian Initiation of Adults (RCIA) program.*

❧ *Holy Family High School Youth Group members take part in Make a Difference Day, a national day sponsored by the diocese, teaching the importance of giving back to the community.*

Hannibal's history of faith spans three centuries from the first celebration of Mass by Fr. Louis Hennepin in 1680 at Bay de Charles. Three Catholic parishes; Immaculate Conception, St. Joseph (New London), Holy Cross (Ilasco), Blessed Sacrament

❧ *Holy Family, Hannibal*

and St. Mary's Churches, each with it's own diversity, now stand as Holy Family Church; embracing our strength as a Catholic, "holy family" of faith.

Catholic Schools have a deep and rich tradition in the Hannibal community. It has been blessed with St. Joseph's Academy, McCooey High School, St. Mary's and Blessed Sacrament Schools. Two congregations of Sisters, the Sisters of St. Joseph and the School Sisters of Notre Dame, have educated many generations of area Catholic families. Their commitment to Catholic education continues as Holy Family School, with students in grades Pre-K-8, flourishes in this growing, faith-filled community.

The dedication and devotion of Holy Family parishioners, past and present, have guided the parish's journey of faith to the present "Body of Christ" in Hannibal.

St. George, Hermann
1845

In 1995 St. George parish celebrated 150 years of being, through the grace of God, a dynamic faith community on the south bank of the Missouri. To be sure, fine priests served the church 30 years before the Franciscans came in 1875 to guide the congregation into the new century, as well as the one following. They designed and decorated the church and continued the school. Fr. Ambrose German, OFM was the last Franciscan pastor. Fr. William Debo, the current pastor, is the first diocesan priest in more than a century. A great debt of gratitude is owed all the priests who ministered in the parish.

ↄ *Stained-glass window: Consolation of the Sick*

ↄ *Interior*

St. George is not merely a beautiful red brick church with awesome windows depicting the corporal and spiritual works of mercy. It is a vibrant continuation of the German Catholic heritage of faith, sacrifice and love of its early congregations.

ↄ *St. George, Hermann, dedicated July 9, 1916*

St. Bernadette, Hermitage
1973

St. Bernadette parish is located in the vicinity of Lake Pomme de Terre in Hickory County. The members of the church run the gamut of ages, from retired people to small children. Being the only Catholic church in Hickory County, it fulfills the need of area residents and the many visitors to the lake.

The parish family is close-knit, yet never failing to welcome new parishioners as well as visitors. The Ladies Guild and St. Stephen Men's Club provide outlets for parish and countywide activities. The Parish Council, consisting of president, administrator, social concerns chair, religious education chair, liturgy committee chair and secretary cares for the everyday operations of the parish.

The first documented Mass in the area was celebrated in the Dame Site Park in November

Lourdes shrine, St. Bernadette before the Blessed Virgin

1973 because of the growing need for pastoral care for lake area residents and visitors. The first church building was constructed by members of the parish and in use by Holy Thursday, April 15, 1976. It was dedicated as St. Bernadette Church on May 16, 1976 by Bishop McAuliffe. The building was expanded in 1984 through the generosity of a parishioner. In 1998/99, under the guidance of Fr. Donald Powers, another addition was completed and dedicated on December 12, 1999, by Bishop John Gaydos bringing the church to its present size and seating capacity of 350 to 400 people.

During the past year the addition of stained-glass windows, designed and executed by a parishioner, has added to the religious ambiance of the church. The almost weekly registration of new members indicates a continuing growth pattern.

St. Bernadette, Hermitage, dedicated May 14, 1976.

St. Andrew, Holts Summit
1975

❧ Interior of St. Andrew Church

❧ Interior of St. Andrew Church

T he Catholic community north of the Missouri River was challenged in 1974 to start a church in Holts Summit. Warning of possible serious difficulties, Fr. John Buchanan, pastor of St. Peter, Jefferson City, asked the community to try. Lacking monetary means for a church, the people came together and built a strong community. The first Mass was held outdoors and was followed by liturgies in a firehouse and civic center.

As parish membership grew, means were found over the next 30 years for the construction of a multi-purpose building. In June 2003, members of the parish proudly and joyfully processed into their new church on dedication day, October 19, 2003.

While the people of St. Andrew have given generously of their time and talents to accomplish their goal, their dream is to achieve their ongoing objective—a Church community alive with the spirit of Christ.

❧ St. Andrew, Holts Summit

🙠 *St. Stephen, Indian Creek, oldest parish in Diocese*

St. Stephen, Indian Creek
1833

🙠 *Parishioners gather at the parish marker after its erection in 1986. Standing far left is Ben Smith, a lifelong member of St. Stephen. Captain Smith gave his life when the helicopter he piloted was shot down in Iraq. He and other parishioners from many previous generations are buried in the cemetery that lies behind the historic "Swinkey Wall."*

The third Sunday of July finds the small community of Indian Creek bustling with activity as the annual Swinkey Picnic is celebrated by parishioners and guests of St. Stephen Parish. During the day, children often sit at the base of the marker noting that the parish, oldest in the Diocese of Jefferson City, was established in 1833 "to nourish the faith of a growing community." Many of those working at the picnic bear the family names of the earliest settlers.

Several church buildings were erected and destroyed by fire and cyclone, but the parish rebuilt and continued. The current church was dedicated on October 3, 1917. More than 5,800 baptisms and 1,000 marriages are noted in the parish records and the parish continues to thrive.

Extensive remodeling of the church and parish hall has recently been completed. Swinkey Days, a summer camp for nearly 100 local children, is planned and staffed by parish youth each July. The local Knights of Columbus Council is also gaining recognition for the fall Corn Maze.

In accord with the mission noted on its historic marker, St. Stephen continues "to nurture the faith of a growing community as it welcomes new members, inviting them to make the parish their own. The rich history and heritage of St. Stephen, the descendants of the early settlers and the gifts and talents of the newcomers combine and flourish in the beautiful rural setting.

🙠 *Sanctuary*

St. Patrick, Jonesburg
1862

From its inception in 1868 to the present, St. Patrick parish has had the outstanding ability to build community spirit. Welcoming parishioners make their parish a true family and home for all who come.

Located in close proximity to Interstate 70, the parish offers Sacraments to the faithful, hospitality to the transient in need and food to many who come for fish fries and dinners for the public.

The parish is alive because of God's Spirit in its people who utilize their gifts to create quality worship, excellent educational programming, expansive social outreach and effective administration and stewardship of resources.

☙ *Sanctuary of St. Patrick*

☙ *St. Patrick Religious Education Students*

☙ *St. Patrick Red Hatters "Over 50 club"*

☙ *St. Patrick, Jonesburg*

☙ *St. Patrick parishioners work behind the scenes*

St. Michael, Kahoka
1891

St. Michael Church began as a mission parish of St. Patrick in St. Patrick, Missouri. The original church was built in 1897. The present church was dedicated on November 15, 1959. With seven young women dedicating their lives as religious, the parish has been fertile ground for religious life.

And Fr. Tom Alber, a native of St. Michael, is currently a priest of the Diocese of Jefferson City.

St. Michael parish serves the northern section of Clark County and has St. Martha's parish as a mission as well as the Shrine of St. Patrick in St. Patrick.

ॐ *St. Michael, Kahoka*

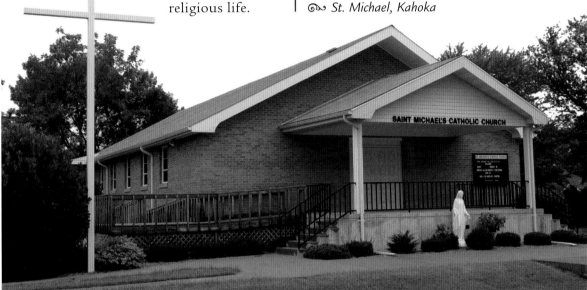

St. Martha, Wayland
1887

St. Martha Church, in the eastern portion of Clark County, was founded in the early 1880s by a mix of native-born members and immigrants from Ireland, Germany and other European countries.

It began as the Assumption of the Blessed Virgin Mary in 1887. The original frame church building was replaced in 1964 through a grant from the Catholic Extension Society and was renamed St. Martha in recognition of the generosity of the family of Martha Fitzgerald. It was dedicated on April 25, 1965.

One parishioner, Anna Fox, entered religious life as a Daughter of Charity and Jerry Lee Arthur entered the Franciscan Friars. St. Martha is a mission parish of St. Michael, Kahoka.

ॐ *St. Martha, Wayland*

Mary Immaculate, Catholic Newman Center, Kirksville

1888

The Newman Club began in 1952 to serve the students at Northeast Missouri State University and Kirksville College of Osteopathic Medicine. They met in the basement of Mary Immaculate Church until 1968 when the first building was purchased at 414 W. Dodson. In 20 years, that space was outgrown and a new building was dedicated in April 1990 at the current location, 709 S. Davis. By 2000 that space was outgrown and an addition was built. The Newman Center continues to serve more than 2000 at the universities of Truman State University and A. T. Still University of Health Sciences.

Newman Center's mission statement proclaims: We, as a Catholic collegiate community, celebrate God with all people by providing numerous opportunities that encourage fellowship and nurture spiritual growth."

A vibrant student council strives to offer a large variety of activities. Many spiritual opportunities are offered, including Eucharistic adoration, rosaries, novenas, retreats and Bible studies. There are two Sunday Masses and two weekday Masses. The social life of the young adults is also fostered by frequent parties, dances and barbeques.

❧ Newman Center

❧ College students display musical and acting talents

❧ Mary Immaculate, Kirksville, dedicated on June 15, 1947

❧ At the Newman Center Coffee House: Lauren Reiss, Laura Hoffman, Jessica Fishering and Angela Wilker

82

St. Rose of Lima, Novinger
1903

St. Rose of Lima, Novinger, was established by Fr. Albert B. Gassd who pastored the church at Kirksville from December 1903 to 1910. Prior to that a church existed at Collinsville four miles north. St. Rose served the growing needs of the Irish, Croation and Italian immigrants in the coal mining business. It was dedicated on October 18, 1905 by Bishop Maurice F. Burke of St. Joseph.

St. Joseph Church, LaPlata, was also a mission served out of Mary Immaculate, Kirksville for many years.

▸ *St. Rose of Lima, Novinger; Mission of Mary Immaculate, Kirksville*

Our Lady of the Lake, Lake Ozark
1940

Our Lady of the Lake parish was established when a quaint stone chapel was completed on November 1, 1942. As visitors to the Lake area increased, so did the crowds at the church. By the summer of 1962, 12 Masses were celebrated each Sunday. The little chapel, which stood on the site of Monarch Plaza, was eventually torn down. The present church and former rectory on its current site replaced it. With the completion of the new church, a resident pastor was assigned to serve the parish at the Lake of the Ozarks.

In 1993 an addition to the existing church provided the parish with a chapel, a fellowship area and needed office space. In 1999 a new rectory was purchased, allowing the old rectory to be used for classrooms.

From a small chapel to a large church that seats 1200, Our Lady of the Lake continues to serve the parishioners, summer residents and visitors to the Ozarks area. While the church has grown in size and membership, the parish has maintained its mission of being a community of faith with a spirit of welcoming to visitors of the area.

CTC youth present a check to Hope House after sleeping out in cardboard boxes to raise funds.

Our Lady of the Lake Chapel, Lake of Ozark. From 1942 to 1966, the Chapel was the center of Catholic life.

Wood sanctuary furnishings contrast against the brick wall of the sanctuary.

Our Lady of the Lake, Lake Ozark, dedicated on March 16, 1980.

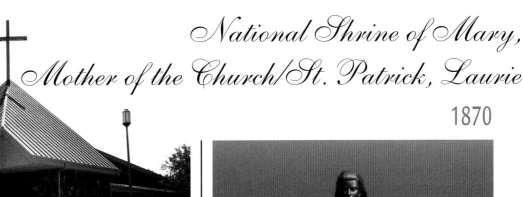

☙ *Statue of Mary, Mother of the Church*

S t. Patrick's parish in Laurie, Missouri, at the beautiful Lake of the Ozarks, is rather unique in that seven Osage Indian Chieftains rode into St. Charles to the home of the Bishop and requested a missionary to minister to them. A Jesuit Belgian Missionary, Father Charles de La Croix, was sent to minister to the Indians, thus beginning Catholicism in this area.

When the Irish immigrants arrived, they felt at home. The green hills of the Ozarks reminded them of the green hills of Ireland and Catholicism was already established. They built the church in 1868.

The last regular church service was held at the Old St. Pat's Cemetery Church, July 20, 1952. It was placed on the National Register of Historic Sites, March 1979. The Knights of Columbus won the prestigious International Service Award for restoration of the old church in 1998. Mass is still celebrated there twice a year.

The second St. Patrick's Church was built in Gravois Mills with an addition added in the 1960's. It served the area until 1980 when the crowds again outgrew this church.

The third St. Patrick's Church, was built just North of Laurie and dedicated on May 24, 1980. By the mid 1980's, the summer crowds were again overflowing the church. Instead of adding on to this church, Father Fred Barnett, pastor, decided to build a little grotto to Mary where Mass could be celebrated.

The little grotto grew into a Shrine and was dedicated in 1988 as Mary, Mother of the Church, the newest title given to Mary at the Second Vatican Council. The sculpture of Mary arrived in 1992. Visitors started flowing into the Shrine and retreats were held regularly. A board was appointed to oversee the Shrine

The Mothers' Wall of Life was added in 1999 as a tribute to motherhood and family life. The Mothers' Wall of Life makes this a most meaningful Shrine.

In 2003, Archbishop Keleher, of the Bishops Committee for National Shrines, and Bishop Gaydos made the announcement to the parishioners that the Mothers Shrine had been designated as the National Shrine of Mary, Mother of the Church.

☙ *Families gather to see how the Wall has grown and who they know on the Mother'Wall of life.*

St. Philip Benizi, Versailles
1963

Scattered among three parishes, Versailles Catholics traveled miles to Mass every Sunday as well as to religious services and instructions. They were never part of any parish, yet they were faithful in preserving the faith their parents had devotedly passed on to them. Finally, in 1962 a small group of people petitioned the bishop to build a church.

The first Mass at St. Philip Benizi church was celebrated on Thanksgiving Day, 1963. It was dedicated on May 24, 1964 by Bishop Marling.

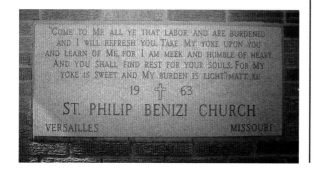

An Altar Guild was formed and the men of the parish began the care of the church grounds. From the beginning, the people of the parish have been active in local community events such as Cross Lines, World Day of Prayer and volunteer work at the nursing and boarding homes. Extraordinary Ministers of Holy Communion are always faithful in bringing Communion to the elderly and sick.

Parish activities include a weekly social hour after Sunday Mass and CCD classes taught by the laity. The Sisters of Charity of Leavenworth directed the religious education program in the parish for a while.

For 44 years the parish has grown in families and important parish traditions. The parish that once was a vision for a few, has become a parish home for many.

Dedication cornerstone of St. Philip church

St. Philip Benizi

St. George, Linn
1866

The original church was as plain and simple as its members. The 75,000 bricks in the building were made in 1866 from the same earth on which the church was built. The cornerstone was laid on Pentecost 1867.

A second church seating 400 that was erected next to the original required 400,000 bricks and its cornerstone was laid in 1894. When it closed in 1974, construction on the current church began. The first Mass was offered in 1976. It was dedicated on May 2, 1976.

The rectory that was completed in 1899 was renovated interiorly in 1986 and exteriorly in 1995. The first convent for the School Sisters of Notre Dame was built in early 1883. There St. George Mission School began in two rooms. The present convent was completed in 1962. Its basement was designed to house the Sewing Circle and the Good Samaritan Food Pantry.

The "old" mission school, built in 1909, has since been renovated and opened as St. George Elementary School in 1955. A Junior High School occupied the second floor of Notre Dame Hall with classes beginning in 1994. Renovations in the building were designed to accommodate funeral dinners, Bingo, parish meetings and a Day Care Center on the basement level. Enrollment currently hovers around 175.

❧ Sanctuary

❧ St. George, Linn

Immaculate Conception, Loose Creek
1845

Immaculate Conception parish of Loose Creek was founded by Fr. Ferdinand Helias in 1835. The present church building was completed in 1877. The congregation at the time was made up of German immigrants who came from the Rhineland area of Germany to settle in Loose Creek. A monument to them on the church lawn that was dedicated in 1992 shows the names and towns from which they originated. It shares this memorial with a sister city in Lank, Germany.

ᧁ *Historic plaque of sister city in Germany*

Loose Creek is famous for the golden fried chicken and German pot roast served at the annual parish picnic held every June.

The parish is also blessed to have a school, which has been served by the School Sisters of Notre Dame since 1891. It is fortunate to have two sisters still teaching and living in the school and parish. In May 2003, Immaculate Conception celebrated its 150th anniversary.

ᧁ *Interior of the Church*

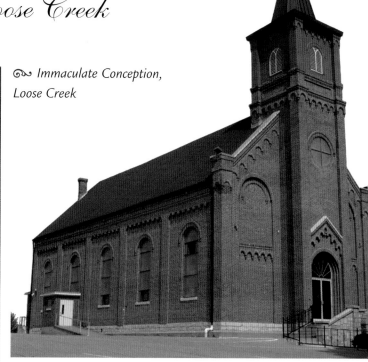

ᧁ *Immaculate Conception, Loose Creek*

ᧁ *Immaculate Conception school children at lunch*

ᧁ *Parish picnic 2004*

ᧁ *Annual Christmas program*

ꙮ *Interior of St. Joseph church*

St. Joseph, Louisiana
1865

The Catholic people of Louisiana built a church in 1850 and had occasional Masses provided by the priest from Milwood. In 1864 the congregation received its first resident pastor and the parish of St. Joseph was formally established in 1865.

The present church was dedicated in 1874.

During the following century, a mission was opened in Elsberry, now a parish in its own right, and in 1951, and another mission, Mary, Queen of Peace, in Clarksville.

The original tall steeple was burned in a fire in 1915 and in falling, caused the rectory to catch fire as well. The rectory was replaced, but not the steeple.

The parish currently registers slightly more than 120 households.

ꙮ *St. Joseph, Louisiana*

Queen of Peace, Clarksville (mission)
1951

A parish existed in Clarksville from 1868 to 1888 under the title of St. Joseph, but, along with its small wood frame church, it faded away.

In 1951 a Catholic mission parish was established in the same area, using a rented storefront as a gathering space for worship.

The congregation was served out of St. Joseph Parish in Louisiana.

In 1953 the parish was attached to Sacred Heart in Elsberry, but after the erection of the new Diocese of Jefferson City, the parish was reattached to Louisiana in 1958. The present church was built in 1955-1956 with the assistance of the Catholic Extension Society. It was dedicated on November 27, 1955, by Cardinal Ritter.

The parish today serves 45 families.

❧ *Queen of Peace, Mission of St. Joseph, Louisiana*

怘 *Immaculate Conception, Macon*

怘 *Stations of the Cross in stained glass*

怘 *Sanctuary with creative and symbolic use of wood*

One of the first priests recorded coming to Macon County was Father John J. Hogan in August of 1857. Monthly services were conducted in homes until 1860 when a small church was erected. The church became a casualty of the Civil War when its pews, altars, and flooring were removed to use as firewood and defense ramparts. In 1865, the church was rebuilt and moved.

A Presbyterian Church served as our first Immaculate Conception Church between 1875 and 1902 when a larger church replaced it. In 1920 the townhouse of Colonel Frederick Blees was purchased. Located on the present church site, the first floor was used as a church with a school and convent on the second floor. The parish purchased a doctor's residence in 1952 located east of the present church. This residence was remodeled and additions made to become the present school building. The parish razed the church and built the present church which was dedicated on May 5, 1957.

During the next years, changes in the liturgy and spirituality according to Vatican II reforms took place. In 1974, the church was redecorated including the installation of the current stained glass windows depicting an inspirational Stations of the Cross. During these years, an increasingly active laity involved themselves in parish council, Oktoberfest, parish fundraisers, Cursillo, Marriage Encounter, and Journey in Faith - spiritual renewal. In 1985, Bernie Toll was ordained Macon's first permanent deacon with Leo Prenger being ordained a deacon in 1989.

Many social and economic challenges have faced the parish over the years. Through the presence of the Holy Spirit, the support of many parishioners and the pastors' leadership, the parish has continued to be a source of faith for Macon County Catholics.

Sacred Heart, Bevier (mission)
1880

The Sacred Heart parish of Bevier was established as a mission parish of Immaculate Conception in Macon sometime in 1880. Father P.B. Cahill first said Mass, in Bevier's Goodale Hall and shortly thereafter a church was built on the site of today's structure.

When Father P. B. Cahill said the first Mass, the names on the parish roster read something like:

Lyng, Mikel, Rafter, Rudy, Spicer, Watson, etc. Then, in 1890, a man named Frank D. Chiarottino moved south of Bevier to work in the then booming coal mine industry. He proved to be the first of an Italian immigration. Following the Chiarottinos came: Amedeis, Amideis, Beltramos, Bertis, Biancos, Biondis, Brugionis, Cervas, Colombattos, Contrattos, Donellis, Formentos, Fraulinis, Lenzinis, Lollis, Marchettis, Marras, Nerinis, Nicolais, Pagliais, Peroglios, Quarcelinos, Riconis, Rivettos, Ronchettos, Seghis, Trucanos, and Zuccarinis. The complexion of the Sacred Heart parish roster was changed forever.

In 1938, because of severe storm damage to the first church building, the present clay brick structure was erected and, amazingly enough considering it was the middle of the "great depression", paid for. That story and the stories of the people who made it happen tell a great deal about one of the few self-supporting mission parishes in the nation.

They began pulling down the old church on the first of March 1938 and with volunteer labor, constructed the basement dug by hand. The dirt was hauled away by horse and wagon. The Bevier merchants announced that they would help cover expenses and the contractor loaned them the use of his cement mixer.

☙ *Sacred Heart, Mission of Immaculate Conception, Macon*

Building churches was certainly not the only parish activity. The Bevier congregation has always tried to maintain as many religious services as possible. The Italian love of a festive occasion has always made May processions, Midnight Mass and Easter mornings something special at Sacred Heart. The Altar Society's Memorial Day Ham Dinner is as well attended as it is famous. Card parties, anniversaries, showers, wedding receptions and dances have kept the church basement a center of community activity.

The Sacred Heart Church stands today as a tribute to a spirit of cooperation, of harmony, of sharing the responsibility, and of sharing the fun.

St. Bonaventure, Marceline

St. Bonaventure parish was founded in 1888 by Bishop John J. Hogan of Kansas City, Missouri, simultaneously with the establishment of the town of Marceline. The church has since been renovated several times, most recently in 2001. Its stained-glass windows have been preserved throughout the years and the life-size statue representing the crucifixion of Our Lord that now hangs in the church was imported from Europe and donated by the Croatian Lodge #150.

St. Bonaventure honored in a stained-glass window

Catholic education was a priority of the parish beginning in 1911 with the construction of St. Rose Hall and continuing until today with the Fr. McCartan Memorial School.

Children bring the gifts to Fr. Jerry Kaimann at the children's Christmas Mass

St. Bonaventure parish has many strong and active organizations and boasts countless volunteers giving of their time and talent. Its annual St. Patrick Festival brings people from miles around to enjoy the good food, games and festivities.

St. Bonaventure, Marceline

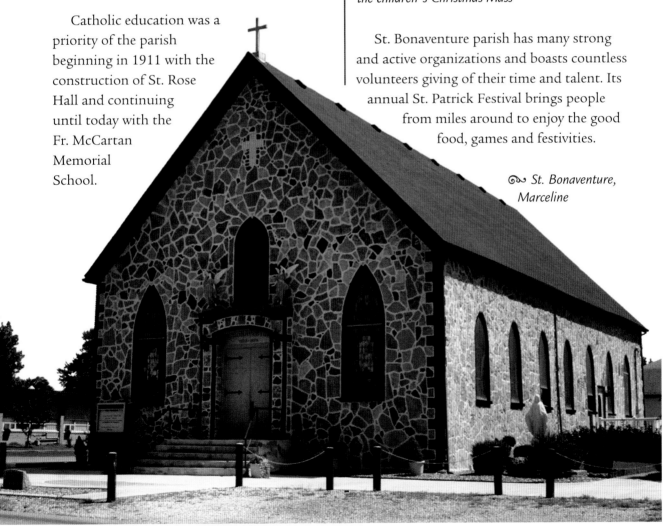

St. Peter, Marshall
1860

In 1851 the first framed church building was erected on the property where St. Mary's Cemetery, Shackelford, stands today. During Fr. John J. Hogan's nine-year tenure, the parish location was changed to Shackelford.

In 1868, Father Hamill organized St. Peter's Parish in Marshall, which had been growing and numbered about 300 Catholics. The first church was built in 1870 at 367 West Arrow.

Father Michael J. O'Dwyer became pastor of St. Peter Parish in Marshall in 1882. He started the first school building in 1883. Mercy Academy was the first co-educational high school in the Diocese of Kansas City. In 1949, St. Peter's Grade School was built. A gymnasium for both grade and high school was added in 1955. In 1958 a new Mercy High School and convent were erected. A second floor was added to the grade school and the gym was enlarged in 1963. The 1988-89 term began with an all-lay staff who pledged to continue the tradition of a fine Catholic school.

As Marshall grew Father James J. O' Sullivan and the Parish Building Committee decided to relocate to the southwest corner of Marshall where 23 acres of farmland were purchased. A new church was dedicated May 1, 1977 by Bishop McAuliffe. The new complex includes a rectory and parish hall.

In 2004, the church was completely renovated with the addition of a pitched roof, bell tower, carillons, and redecoration of the interior, all at a cost of $900,000. Funding came from a $1.5 million Capital Campaign to renovate church, school, parish hall and rectory.

Because of the decline in the membership of Immaculate Conception as well as in the number of available priests in the Jefferson City Diocese, the Shackelford Parish closed July 30. 1977.

In recent years there has been a large influx of Hispanics to the Marshall community. A diocesan priest provides a Mass in Spanish two Sundays in the month.

 St. Peter, Marshall

Holy Family, Sweet Springs
1860

❧ *Holy Family, Sweet Springs; Mission of St. Peter, Marshall, dedicated November 21, 1982*

Holy Family Parish, in Sweet Springs was established in the 1940s as a Mission parish served by the pastor of Immaculate Conception. The mission was closed for a few years. The number of Catholic families increased again, and the church was reopened under the care of the St. Peter Parish.

In 1981 an exchange of property was negotiated with Berg Mortuaries of Sweet Springs, and the Church grounds and building were sold to the Bergs in exchange for a newer building that had been a funeral chapel and residence. The chapel was remodeled in 1982 and serves today as a fitting place of worship under the patronage of the Holy Family. It has both a Parish Council and a religious education program.

❧ *Interior of Holy Family Church*

❧ *Beautiful wood-carved tabernacle*

St. Joseph, Martinsburg
1860

Martinsburg, was founded on the North Missouri Railroad built by Irish Catholic labor in 1857. The first house was home to a section boss and the town's first Mass was celebrated in that Irish Catholic home. The real drive to St. Joseph's becoming a viable parish, however, came from the German immigrants. They began arriving on the Grand Prairie in the 1870s at the urging of a Catholic priest who was preaching the availability of good farmland. It was not long before these settlers wanted their own church rather than be served as a mission of other towns.

> Bishop John R. Gaydos joins Deacon Vincent Garufi and Father Wayne Boyer for Mass to celebrate the interior restoration of St. Joseph Church in Martinsburg in 2002.

The choice of a name for St. Joseph Parish was influenced by the fact that a good number of homesteaders came from St. Joseph Parish in Westphalia, Missouri. They also brought with them an idea of utmost importance, their belief in Catholic education. The Catholic school became the backbone of parish life. That value remains today. Out of this solid education grew vocations to both the priesthood and religious life. Some families sent their children to other Catholic institutions, such as to the Christian Brothers in St. Louis after they had completed the course at St. Joseph's.

> Statue of St. Joseph on the church property

> Interior of the Church

The local school is especially honored to have been the training ground of Maryknoll Bishop Adolph Paschang, the "Little Bishop of Charity" who was always proud of being from Martinsburg and its church.

A basic blessing that helped the church flourish was the foundation for success laid by its first two pastors, Frs. Haar and Freese. Between them they gave 68 years of faithful service. St. Joseph supports the mission Church of the Resurrection, Wellsville.

St. Joseph Church takes pride in its legacy and looks forward to future challenges with faith-based anticipation.

> St. Joseph, Martinburg

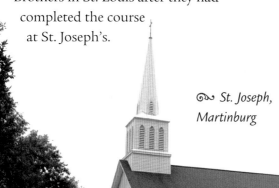

Resurrection, Wellsville
1873

Resurrection Parish of Wellsville was formed about 1873. Mass was celebrated in homes of parishioners and in a town hall. A building site was purchased and a frame church was built. Because the cornerstone was laid on Easter 1881, the church was named for the Resurrection.

A school was added in 1922, serving until 1935. In 1949 it was converted to a parish hall.

Fr. Joseph Murray, pastor from 1928 to 1953, donated Our Lady of Lourdes Grotto honoring parishioners who served during World War II. In February 1954 the parish hall was made the church and the old church, torn down.

Resurrection has the distinction of having had twin brothers Frs. Severin and Stephen Lamping as pastors.

Resurrection Parish, now a mission of St. Joseph, Martinsburg, has an active PSR program, CWO and an Annual Pancake and Sausage Breakfast.

Resurrection Church, Wellsville

Our Lady of the Snows, Mary's Home
1883

🔖 *Sanctuary from the choir loft*

🔖 *Our Lady of the Snows, Mary's Home*

🔖 *The Eucharist honored in a stained-glass window*

In the late 1800s, German Catholic settlers lived in a quiet community area. They were served by a Precious Blood Father, Cosmas Seeberger, who forded the Osage River each week from St. Elizabeth, Missouri, to serve the congregation.

The community built its first church in 1883, calling it St. Mary. Robert Morgan, the local tavern and landowner, was helping the area procure its first post office. By his persuasion, the people decided to name their new town Morgan. The following Sunday, the good priest pounded the pulpit insisting that he had founded the town and it would be named Mary's Home. Thus was born the town's name.

In 1889 the first parish school was built. In 1892 the diocese took over the parish from the Precious Blood Fathers. A newly decorated wood frame church burned to the ground January 1, 1907. The people banded together, mined the stone from their land, and built the present stone church, setting the cornerstone June 20, 1907. A few years later the steeple blew off in a tornado. It was replaced through the generosity of former parishioner Fredonia Arens in 2005, almost 100 years later. In 1938 Fr. John Knoebbe changed the parish name from St. Mary to Our Lady of the Snows and wrote the beautiful hymn still sung in her honor.

In 1951 a larger brick school building was completed. Religious sisters operated the school until the Great Depression, when lay teachers took over. In 1957, the sisters returned until 1975 when lay teachers again took charge. A fund drive has been launched to add classrooms and a gym.

🔖 *Quilters of 40 Quilts for the annual Parish Picnic*

St. John LeLand, Memphis
1952

In early 1952, Fr. Mel Newman, of St. Mary of Adair said the first Mass in Memphis in a private home. For the next five years, through the hard work of the people and the encouragement of Fr. Newman, an upper room on the square was secured for the fledgling community. Along with two refrigerator boxes that served as confessionals, donations from neighboring parishes gave the chapel its Catholic character. In 1955 Bishop Cody gave permission to buy land and build a church.

By 1957, with the creation of a new diocese headed by Bishop Marling, the Memphis church was built and consecrated as St. John LeLand Church in response to the request of the Extension Society, which donated $10,000 to the building of the church. In 1995, the windows in the church were replaced with stained glass, creating a wonderful sense of prayerfulness. The serenity of the parish was tested by two very challenging events. In 1998, 100-mile-an-hour winds tore the roof from the trailer that served as both rectory and church office. On New Year's Eve, 1999, a fire essentially destroyed the inside of the church. Mass was celebrated in the fire station, the funeral home and the Methodist Church. Easter 2000 marked the first liturgical celebrations in the totally renovated church. It sparkled with new life and hope that carries on today. These two calamities have served to draw the St. John community closer together and deepened a connection with the community-at-large.

Located ten miles from the Iowa border, St. John serves three counties in two states. The parish has worked hard to gain a foothold in a predominantly non-Catholic area. Over the years St. John has become a well-respected religious spiritual presence in Scotland County.

St. John, Memphis, dedicated on October 20, 1957

St. Cecilia, Meta
1904

The town of Meta, roughly 25 miles south of the capital city, began as a shipping facility for the Rock Island Railroad, was incorporated in 1902 and soon became a small and thriving valley town. Fr. Wagener was sent to minister to the largely Catholic population in the fall of 1904. A school was constructed and Mass was celebrated there until 1906 when the first church, St. Cecilia, was built. A parochial school was established in the schoolhouse and taught by lay teachers and Fr. Wagener.

In 1925 a tornado damaged the 74-foot steeple, causing the clapboard building to sway precariously. In 1928 Fr. Schmalle followed Fr. Wagener and made many improvements, removing the steeple in 1929 and replacing it with a belfry. He engaged the School Sisters of Notre Dame to teach the children of the more than 100 families that now formed the congregation. A convent was completed in 1931. Fr. Hoegen who followed Fr. Schmalle in 1932 served as pastor for 26 years. In 1932 the Sisters of the Most Precious Blood were engaged to teach after the departure of the Notre Dame sisters.

Statue of St. Cecilia, patroness of the parish

Despite renovations in 1933, the church building continued to deteriorate until in 1943 the Archbishop of St. Louis granted permission to build a new church. Construction began, but the project fell victim to the illness and

Sanctuary

death of the first builders, the enlistment of many men either in defense plants or the armed services during World War II, years of economic depression and drought and flooding. Finally in January 1950 construction resumed and the new church was dedicated on April 29, 1951 by Archbishop Ritter.

At the coming of Fr. Wilberding in 1958, a new rectory and school were constructed. With his departure in 1966 the sisters left the parish and the school closed.

After 1988, the interior of St. Cecilia Church was completely renovated using the marble and metalwork already part of the building. The church was rededicated on July 31, 1994 and celebrated its centennial in 2004. Presently 175 families are registered with 75 children enrolled in the CCD program.

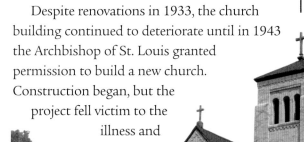

Rectory built in 1960

St. Cecilia, Meta, constructed in 1951

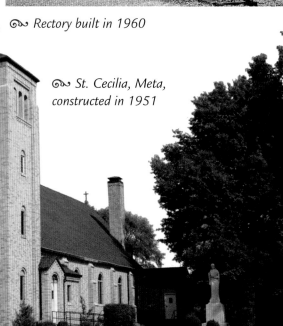

🙠 *Interior of the church*

St. Brendan, Mexico
1857

In 1921 Msgr. Patrick Gavan came on a temporary assignment that lasted 43 years. Under his leadership, a parochial school was started and a new rectory and church were constructed.

The first Mass was offered in Mexico in the home of Thomas Fagan on October 27, 1857, by Fr. John Hogan who was later to become a bishop.

The first church was not built until 1866 and was named for St. Stephen. It was not until 1878 that the parish name was changed to St. Brendan, probably because most of the parishioners were Irish, many of them immigrants who came to build the railroad.

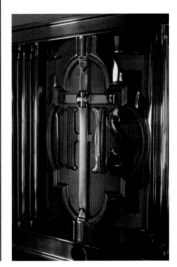

Ever since its foundation, a strong commitment to Catholic education and family spirituality have been hallmarks of St. Brendan parish.

🙠 *Close up of the rich tabernacle door*

🙠 *St. Brendan, Mexico, dedicated on October 27, 1957*

St. Mary, Milan
1868

Bishop John J. Hogan celebrated the first Mass at Milan for Irish settlers on May 19, 1868 in the home of Dennis Ryan. Although it was the first visit of a priest since the immigrants arrived 30 years before, many children and young adults were so well instructed that they could be received into the church without delay.

In 1870 the first resident pastor at Unionville served the area, offering Mass in the Ryan home until St. Mary, a frame church in Milan was dedicated in 1882. Franciscans from Chillicothe attended the church from 1883 to 1887. About 1890 Fr. William F. Hanly, who built the rectory for $300, became the first resident pastor, serving Unionville as its mission. The increase in railroad shops brought growth to the town and improvements in the church and rectory. A new rectory was built in 1908 and St. Mary took on Novinger, Connelsville and Mendota as missions.

☙ *Altar sculpture*

St. Mary celebrated its centennial in 1968. The church was extensively renovated shortly after and now serves all of Putnam County with some 50 Catholic families.

☙ *Sanctuary*

☙ *St. Mary, Milan, dedicated on May 30, 1923*

St. Mary, Unionville
1868

Irish settlers who came to Ohio and Indiana in the 1840s migrated to the Green Hills of north Missouri in the 1850s. By 1865 the number of Catholics was large enough to seek a priest to care for their spiritual needs.

The first recorded Mass in Putnam County was offered by Fr. John J. Hogan (later Bishop Hogan) and Fr. R. S. Tucker at Clarksburg. Services were held in the home of Patrick O'Reilly who labored to raise funds for a new church. For most Catholics of the area, it was the first visit by a priest since they first settled. Many children and adults were baptized and received their First Communion. Fr. J.J. Kennedy became the first resident pastor at Unionville in 1870. Patrick OReilly's eldest son William was ordained for the Diocese of Peoria about the same year.

The first Catholic Church in Unionville was erected by Fr. Kennedy in 1871. Most of the land and gifts were donated by other than Catholics, especially Col. W. William Shelton. Fr. Francis Smyth succeeded Fr. Kennedy in 1875, dying of small pox contracted while caring for the sick. Church records were burned to avoid contagion. Fr. William Hanley, the first

resident pastor, died of pneumonia in 1880. He was 29. Fr. J.J. Jermain, who built the rectory in 1907, was electrocuted when he ran into a live wire near his home in Milan.

Unionville celebrated its centennial in 1968 during the pastorate of Fr. George Kramer. He was succeeded by Fr. Raphael O'Malley who supervised the extensive renovation of St. Mary. Funds for the project were procured from the Sina Faye Fowler estate and the Walter V. Egan memorial Fund.

Unionville is the county seat of Putnam County and St. Mary's serves the 49 Catholic households in the county.

St. Mary, Unionville; Mission of St. Mary, Milan

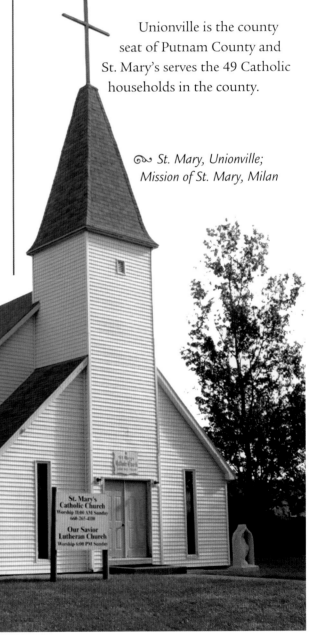

St. Pius X, Moberly
1888

"I love this Church!" These words written by 17-year-old Krissy Koehly in preparation for Confirmation in May 2005 sum up the attitude Moberly Catholics have held since 1870. That love has helped the parish, now known as St. Pius, survive and thrive over the past 130 years.

Moberly began in 1870 under the pastorate of Fr. Francis McKenna. For five years a log cabin served as the first church, St. John the Baptist. In 1877 the Sisters of Loretto from Kentucky began St. Mary's Academy, a Catholic high school for girls. The following year a boys' school opened in a two-room attachment.

A second parish (Immaculate Conception) was started in 1888 with its school opening in 1895. The two parishes and their parochial schools combined in 1955 as St. Pius X.

In 1946, the church was completely destroyed by fire. In 1987 arson again did extensive damage to the church. On Palm Sunday 1988, Bishop McAuliffe blessed the completely restored church. On July 4, 1995, a tornado severely damaged the church, school, rectory and convent, while completely destroying the parish center and offices. Once again, huge contingents of parish volunteers rebuilt the church and other damaged parish buildings.

ⓖ *Sanctuary*

In the late 1990s, St. Pius School underwent a $2.2 million expansion, including a new gym and an Early Childhood Center. In 2003 Perpetual Adoration was launched with more than 200 parishioners praying round the clock. New security was added after an armed robbery in 2004, with adorers coming forward in even greater numbers afterward. Volunteers rebuilt the church undercroft destroyed by a Labor Day flood in 2003. The Knights of Columbus also dedicated a new building.

Today St. Pius serves nearly 500 families. The parish school and Early Childhood Center train 270 children.

ⓖ *Adoration Chapel*

ⓖ *St. Pius X, Moberly*

St. Jude Thaddeus, Mokane
1900

Mass was celebrated in Mokane beginning in 1900. Fr. George W. Hoehn, pastor at Starkenburg, Missouri, traveled by train once a month to offer Mass in a room at the Yoest Hotel. Fr. Hoehn was the first priest assigned to St. Jude Thaddeus Church when it was built in 1909. The church was formerly established as a mission of St. Peter Church in Fulton in 1910. The basement was hand dug by parishioners in 1947, and the expansion of the Church in 1966 doubled the size of the original building. St. Jude Thaddeus was erected as an independent parish in 1969.

🕭 *Cassandra Kiera crowns the Blessed Mother at an outdoor shrine.*

St. Jude parish family is a beautiful mixture of lifelong parish members and new parishioners who have moved to the area. Most are farmers and blue-collar workers. Some are nurses, bankers and nuclear power plant workers. All, except the farmers, commute to their place of employment. The parish consists of 60 households that vary in age.

The Missouri River, many lakes and ponds, the Katy trail and scenic views from rolling hills provide recreation and enjoyment as well as a source of prayerful praise to God in thanksgiving for the wonders of creation. For more than 100 years this small Catholic church has been a steadfast witness of Catholic faith and morals to the community.

🕭 *The sanctuary*

🕭 *St. Jude choir members*

🕭 *St. Jude Thaddeus, Mokane*

Holy Rosary, Monroe City
1884

✍ *Interior of Holy Rosary church*

Holy Rosary Parish, Monroe City, was founded in 1884 to serve English/Irish settlers from Maryland and Kentucky, some of whom traced their faith back to the renowned English martyr, Edmund Campion.

In 1901 Fr. Sullivan became the first resident pastor and built the first school, inviting the Sparkhill Dominicans to staff it. A Dominican sister has been principal ever since, including the current principal, Sr. Suzanne Walker, a native of the parish.

In 1919 Msgr. Connolly arrived as pastor of Holy Rosary, a position he held for 55 years, serving in three different dioceses without moving from Holy Rosary! He built the present school, which included a high school until it closed in 1966 after graduating a total of 668 students. Holy Rosary Elementary School remains strong and vibrant with 150 pupils. It has a reputation for excellence in academics and strong faith values.

In 1969 under Fr. Ludwig, a new, white brick church campus was built. It was dedicated on May 18, 1969. It comprised a church, a rectory and a convent. The Knights of Columbus added a spacious new KC parish hall in 1997.

Holy Rosary assumed responsibility for St. Peter at Brush Creek in the late 1960s. Its church was built in 1862 and is on the National Register of Historic Places as the site of the Baptism of the first recognized African-American Catholic priest in the United States, Fr. Augustine Tolton. Mass is celebrated there twice yearly.

Since 1985 in partnership with nearby St. Stephen in Indian Creek, Holy Rosary has sustained and benefited from a Perpetual Adoration ministry. A vibrant parish community, Holy Rosary has a history of strong lay leadership with members active in Cursillo, REC, TEC, Lay ministry classes, Disciples in Mission groups and centering prayer groups. Its Parish Council, its Commissions and its Stewardship Committee are active and vital. The Knights of Columbus, Daughters of Isabella, Altar Society and PTO contribute in significant ways in building the faith community of Holy Rosary.

✍ *Holy Rosary, Monroe City*

Immaculate Conception, Montgomery City
1861

Immaculate Conception is the parish home of Catholics residing in the Montgomery City area and beyond. Members include those who have long lines of membership and service in the parish and those who have more recently moved into the community and enthusiastically become active in the life of the parish.

The foundation of Immaculate Conception was laid in 1842 when Mass was first celebrated in the home of Charles Worland. The first church was built in 1861 and the current church was dedicated July 3, 1887. The parish elementary school opened about the time the first church was built, closed in the early 1970s and reopened in 1991.

Highlight annual parish events include a Parish Mission, Prime Rib Dinner, Parish Picnic, Epiphany Party and Golf Tournament.

The parish community at Sunday Eucharist

Immaculate Conception school children on Field Day

Parish picnic

Immaculate Conception, Montgomery City

The parish regularly participates in ecumenical activities and many parishioners are active in their local communities in positions of leadership and service, making Immaculate Conception Parish a vital part of Montgomery County.

Assumption, Morrison
1875

In 1853 a priest from Hermann began visiting a few families near Gasconade. It was later decided to build a new church at Morrison as most of the parishioners lived in and around that area.

Assumption Church in Morrison was dedicated on August 28, 1875. The present church building served as a school from 1958 when it was built until 1964 when the school closed.

In 1970 the building was converted into the present parish church. In the flood of 1993, the church was inundated by flash flood water. Completely remodeled, it was rededicated in August 1994.

 ⤶ *Bishop Michael F. McAuliffe rededicates Most Pure Heart of Mary Church in Chamois in 1994.*

⤶ *Parishioners assemble for Mass*

St. Margaret of Antioch, Osage Bend

1907

A t the request of 23 families in Osage Bend, Archbishop Glennon of St. Louis established St. Margaret of Antioch Parish in 1907. The first Mass was celebrated in the original wooden church on November 1 that same year. The first parish picnic was held on July 22, 1907.

In conjunction with the 50th anniversary of the parish, which had more than doubled in size to 50 families, the current church was dedicated on September 29, 1957 by Bishop Marling. When by 1982, on its 75th anniversary the parish had increased to 89 families, the current parish hall, completed in 1979, was ready. St. Margaret has not had a resident pastor since 1979 and has been served by pastoral administrators for the past 26 years.

As a result of storm damage to the church, in May 2003 parish families donated new stained-glass windows. The parish faith community continues to grow and presently consists of 138 families. St. Margaret of Antioch Parish will celebrate its 100th anniversary in 2007.

Church interior

Parish Hall, Fry Shack & Prayer Garden

Parish Rectory

St. Margaret of Antioch, Osage Bend

Immaculate Conception, Owensville
1893

◈ *Immaculate Conception*

The seed of a Catholic presence in Owensville can be traced to the apostolic work of Jesuit Fr. P. J. Verhagen in 1830. However, it was under the guidance of another dedicated Jesuit priest, Fr. Alex Mathausheck, that two immigrant communities, setting aside their separate ethnic Polish and Bohemian backgrounds, agreed to establish a united Catholic parish under the patronage of Mary of the Immaculate Conception in 1892.

◈ *Holy Water Font*

Since then, the children and the grandchildren of the first generation of immigrants from Poland and Bohemia have struggled to move forward without losing their roots in their adaptation to the constantly changing modern world.

The current church was built and dedicated on May 14, 1950. A new parish building in 1985 assured continuation of the Catholic faith in the area.

Some of the original family names like Scego, Piezuch, Skornia and Fisher are still on the parish roster, along with the descendants of the Filla, Mertl and Zeman families. The list is

◈ *Immaculate Conception*

◈ *Parishioners of Immaculate Conception, circa 1894*

blessed with other family names like Plassmeyer, Lairmore, Lenauer, Feagan and Jahnsen and many, many more. As they did more than 100 years ago, the parish families of Mary of the Immaculate Conception still seek divine wisdom for the gift of unity, that the name of Jesus may be preached and made effectively present in Owensville.

St. Joseph, Palmyra
1866

In 1680, Father Louis Hennepin, a Franciscan priest explorer from France, raised a cross and offered Mass on the banks of the Mississippi waters, which he named Bay de Charles, claiming the land for France. It was 1818 before any permanent settlers filtered into the present Palmyra parish. Few were Catholics, yet those who came formed a devout foundation for the local church. In 1866 the parish was founded and the two-story wagon shop of Price & Jackson on the west side of Lane Street was

St. Joseph, Palmyra

purchased for $300 and converted into a church. During this period the church was ministered by the Franciscan priests from Saint Francis, Solanus, Parish in Quincy, Illinois. In March 1869, fund raisers were undertaken for the construction of a new church. In May 1899, the cornerstone was laid for the current church building. It was dedicated on November 30, 1899.

The school was built in 1879. The Benedictine Sisters from Atchison, Kansas, staffed the school until 1970 when it closed. The original school was remodeled into the current rectory in 1919, when the new school was completed. After the school closed, the old building was replaced with a new parish hall in 1974. The hall was enlarged in 2000 to include parish offices, meeting rooms and classrooms.

The hall is named for Msgr. Hubert J. Farischon, the first resident pastor. He was appointed pastor on August 4, 1916, and guided the parish for 52 years from 1916 to 1968!

Interior of St. Joseph Church

St. William, Perry - St. Paul, Center
1901

St. Paul was designated as a parish in 1829. It is known as "The Mother Church of the Roman Catholic Faith in Northeastern Missouri, Southeast Iowa and Western Illinois."

St. Paul's church building was placed on the National Register of Historic Places on May 31, 1979. St. Paul Cemetery is the oldest cemetery on record in Ralls County with burials from the Revolutionary War.

The Faith Commmunity that exists in and around Perry had its beginnings more than a century ago in 1901 when it became a mission of St. Paul Church in rural Center. Records indicate that Matthew Elliott, James Keenan and Michael Fitzpatrick deeded the land for St. William in 1966.

The parishes in Perry and Paris each have maintained a steady and faithful membership and are proud to be "the churches away from home" to the many Catholic tourists who visit Mark Twain Lake and other local attractions throughout the year. Sincere and lasting friendships have developed among the parishioners and the weekend visitors forming a true Faith Community in action.

❧ *Stained-glass window of Jesus Teaching by the Sea*

❧ *Church interior*

❧ *St. William, Perry, dedicated on October 12, 1958*

St. Frances Cabrini, Paris
1953

In May 1952, Fr. P. J. Gannon wrote to Bishop Charles H. LeBlond of St. Joseph, Missouri, about building a church in Paris. Permission was granted and eight acres at the southwest edge of Paris were purchased from Claud and Rose Williamson. The church would be a mission attached to the Indian Creek Parish.

The church was dedicated October 11, 1953, by Monsignor Thomas Cusack, pastor of St. Peter Church, Quincy, Illinois. It was placed under the patronage of St. Frances Cabrini, the first United States citizen to be canonized.

The church became a misson of St. William

Church in Perry in 1966 and is served by the same pastor, Fr. John A. Henderson, who was appointed in July 2002.

The Church has enjoyed the influx of many visitors through its proximity to the Mark Twain Lake, as well as the addition of new members. A church choir has been formed, providing special music for Easter and Christmas liturgies. The musical talent of a regular cantor enhances the Sunday celebrations. A new, handicapped-accessible ramp was installed in 2004. Through the enthusiasm of several adult leaders, a vibrant youth group has emerged and has participated in many innovative projects, not the least of which was the Seder Meal at the parish during Holy Week 2005. The Faith Community of St. Frances Cabrini has much to be proud of and is thankful for the blessings that Almighty God has bestowed upon them.

᎒ *Blessed Virgin Mary Shrine set in wooded acreage of the church property*

᎒ *St. Frances Cabrini, Paris; Mission of St. William, Perry*

St. Joseph, Pilot Grove
1894

The Pilot Grove area was first settled in 1820 and was incorporated as a town in 1873. The first Church services were held beneath the canopy of the open sky, then in rude cabins, huts and farmers' homes. Then, in 1893, St. Joseph Catholic Church was organized by Fr. John Conrad from St. John's in Clear Creek.

A school staffed by the Benedictine Sisters opened soon thereafter. The school and parish flourished. Parish societies of St. Joseph, St. Anne, the Holy Name and the Holy Childhood were developed. A two-year high school program was begun in the early 1920s and lasted for several years.

The current Church is actually the third parish church built by 1952. It was dedicated on May 10, 1956. While simple in style, it has a beauty that lends grace and elegance to the many services that take place within its walls.

The history of St. Joseph's Parish would not be complete without recognizing the four other church communities that have merged with the parish over the decades. The communities of Nelson, Martinsville, Clear Creek and, most recently, Clifton City have clustered to comprise today's parish family of St. Joseph. For more

ᘒ *Stained-glass window of Jesus calling the disciples*

ᘒ *Interior of the church*

than 165 years, the Catholic Church has been a part of the lives of the people of Cooper County. A generous supply of hard work and sacrifice has made it the vibrant parish it is today.

ᘒ *St. Joseph, Pilot Grove*

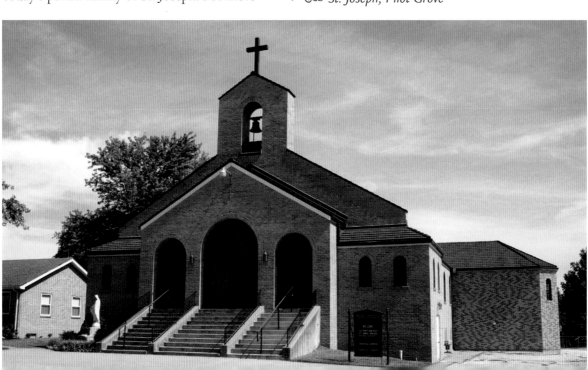

114

The Church of the Risen Savior, Rhineland

1979

☙ *Church of the Risen Savior, Rhineland*

S t. Martin Parish was chartered in 1848. The parish was named after St. Martin, Bishop of Tours, France. One year later 40 acres were obtained and a log church was built on the site. In 1872 parishioners began to replace the log church with one of stone. In 1873, a cornerstone was laid for the new St. Martin Church. In 1891 a 125-foot steeple with two large bells was added.

Near the end of 1891 Fr. Hoehn applied for a post office. He needed to include a name on the forms. Looking around at the hills and the new church steeple, he was reminded of the Starkenburg fortress atop a hill in his German homeland of Heppenheim. In signing "Starkenburg" on the post office form, he in fact named the area. The existing hall at Starkenburg was built in 1964 to serve as a dining hall for pilgrims attending the annual pilgrimages.

St. Joseph Parish was chartered in 1913 after two failed attempts to establish the church in 1848 and then again in 1895. Construction began in 1913 and the dedication was in 1914. The church was expanded in 1932.

The existing St. Joseph Hall was built in 1941. It served as an elementary school for the parish until 1970 when the school closed. It continues to be used as a hall for parish functions.

In 1979 the parishes of St. Martin and St. Joseph were combined to form the Church of the Risen Savior.

SHRINE OF OUR LADY OF SORROWS

In 1906 parishioners began to quarry stone for the Shrine of Our Lady of Sorrows. On July 28, 1906, Fr. Hoehn broke ground, the site was leveled and excavation for the foundation began. The first stone was lowered on October 23 on the Feast of the Holy Redeemer, whom St. Paul called, "the beginning and cornerstone."

The Shrine was dedicated September 15, 1910, with hundreds of pilgrims in attendance by Archbishop Glennon.

☙ *Interior of Risen Savior church*

Sacred Heart, Rich Fountain
1838

Sacred Heart Parish, Rich Fountain was founded in 1838 by Father Ferdinand Helias d'Huddeghem, S.J. The earliest parishioners from Bavaria, Germany, were staunch Catholics, cherishing a faith that has been a "rich fountain" of encouragement and inspiration unto the present generation.

Fr. Helias celebrated the first known Mass for four early Catholic families on May 16, 1838. Within two years the families of Struemph's Settlement had built a small log church on the four acres of land donated by Struemph where the first Mass was celebrated on December 3, 1840. It is thought that the Belgian Fr. Helias renamed the community Riche Fontaine, from the active spring located at the bottom of the church hill. In the early 1850's the parish covered a large part of Osage County, all of Maries County, and also included Durban's Settlement, the present town of Bland. By 1880 the first Mass was celebrated in a new, spacious and artistic church built chiefly by parishioners. It was dedicated on October 16, 1880.

A small log school went up in 1844 and in 1883 the School Sisters of Notre Dame began a ministry that, except for 1891 to 1893, has continued to the present. They received a convent in 1888, which was replaced in 1961. A rectory was added in 1892. The school functioned until a new limestone edifice

replaced it in 1904, and the present brick building was erected in 1964.

Today the Knights of Columbus, St. Ann's Sodality and the Quilting Ladies are active organizations. Annual events that bring many back home to Rich Fountain are the Corpus Christi processions, the annual picnic and quilt auction in summer. The parish currently numbers more than 262 families, many with the same surnames as the first four families. Sacred Heart has given 40 vocations to the Church.

✍ *Painting of the Nativity*

✍ *Interior of the church from the choir*

✍ *Sacred Heart, Rich Fountain*

St. Jude, Richland
1972

St. Jude Parish, Richland, is situated at the edge of the diocese. Until 1972 the people living there went to the surrounding parishes. The founding pastor worked with the 87 interested Catholics to build a parish. Forty-seven people attended the first Mass on June 17, 1972. The parish had a parish council before a parish building. The United Methodist Church building was the first place of worship. The Altar Society began October 24 with 13. Pitch-in dinners, held every year, brought the parish together to celebrate the good work being done and to help solidify plans for the future.

Lack of funds did not deter the people from acquiring land and continuing plans to build.

In the midst of many difficulties and setbacks, including that the building was not finished, the parish moved to celebrate its first Mass on August 24, 1974. That year, through the moving of a trailer from St. Robert parish in St. Robert, St. Jude found a resident pastor for the first time. It was dedicated on April 6, 1975. It required many workdays to clean the land and finish the church interior.

Finally St. Jude was built and it continues to thrive in two ways, in its physical building and its people. It started from a desire to have a church. Then it took the Vatican II documents to heart by living the teaching that people are really the Church and the church building is what the people only use to proclaim the Good News.

St. Jude, Richland

St. Patrick, Rolla
1862

ꙮ *Interior of St. Patrick Church*

ꙮ *Baptismal Pool*

St. Patrick parish was founded in 1862 when Father Patrick Gallagher arrived to minister to the Irish Catholic railroad workers who had settled in Rolla. The original church building, located at Seventh and State Streets, was the first building in Rolla to be built exclusively for religious services. In the early 1940's plans began for construction of a new church to meet the needs of a growing congregation, and on March 9, 1947, under the leadership of Father Lambert, a beautiful new Carthage stone church was dedicated at Highway 63 and St. Patrick Lane. The school was completed in 1953 and the parish hall was constructed in 1975.

ꙮ *Statue of St. Patrick, church patron*

The church was extensively remodeled in 1979 and a pipe organ installed in 1984. Forty-five years after the construction of the church, because of growth in the parish, Father Donald Antweiler planned for further expansion of the church. The work was completed in 1992. The beautiful stone exterior and wood-beamed ceilings were preserved and much of the original wood and stained-glass windows were used in the expanded Church. Both the contractor and the architect had a father or grandfather who had been involved in the construction of the "old" church in 1947.

One of the most beautiful physical attributes of the church is the wonderful Emil Frei stained-glass window that depicts St. Patrick and is mounted in the chapel wall. This window, originally in the church at its State Street location, was moved when the new church was built, and as a result of the remodeling in 1992, was moved yet again to its current location.

St. Patrick Church is privileged to have as its missions St. Patrick School (Pre-3 through 8th grade) and the Catholic Campus Ministry (Newman) Center, now located in a new building dedicated in November 2003.

Many parish organizations promote faith and worship and an active food pantry meets the needs of area's marginalized people. These many missions of faith provide a wonderful source of spirituality and strength among the parishioners and are seen as the work of Christ in the Church today.

ꙮ *St. Patrick, Rolla*

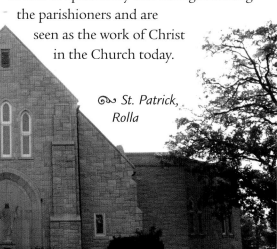

CARDINAL NEWMAN CATHOLIC CAMPUS MINISTRY CENTER
University of Missouri – Rolla

Engaging Life, Proclaiming Faith

Campus Ministry at Rolla began in 1953 under the guidance of Msgr. Gerold Kaiser. Through the years the campus ministry program has served thousands of students who attended the Missouri School of Mines and the University of Missouri-Rolla. A new campus ministry center was dedicated in 2003 as part of the 50th anniversary celebration. The Newman Center currently serves more than 5,000 students by providing opportunities for faith development, fellowship, leadership training, spiritual formation, vocational discernment and service.

❧ *Lunchtime at Rolla Newman Center*

For many students the Newman Center becomes a home away from home and a place where faith becomes their own during challenging college years. The Newman Center, closely affiliated with St. Patrick parish in Rolla, is a place of discernment, a community of faith and an experience of life.

❧ *Specially designed stained-glass window in the Incarnate Word Chapel at the Rolla Newman Center*

❧ *Rolla Newman Center*

St. Anthony, Rosati
1908

Rosati, Missouri, originally named Knobview, was settled by a group of Italian immigrants in the late 1880s.

~ *Interior of St. Anthony Church*

The first church was built in 1906. It was named Chiesa di Sant' Antonio di Padoua, St. Anthony of Padua. Fr. Ottavio Leone was the first pastor and early church records were written in Italian. This church burned in 1918.

A second church, opened a year later, burned in 1946 and in 1947 was replaced by a brick structure, which stands today.

~ *St. Anthony shrine*

Many of the present parishioners are descendants of the original Italian immigrants. The current parish is alive and active. Nestled in the midst of rich grape vineyards, it is known for its annual spaghetti dinners.

~ *Vera Pizza, Chetty Pordee, Scotti Favvzza, Corrine Zulpo, Julie Marchi and Ricard Cordetti prepare the pasta for the spaghetti dinner.*

~ *St. Anthony Church*

Interior of St. Michael Church

St. Michael, Russellville
1906

On October 15, 1887, $100 was donated for a parcel of land deeded to Russellville to establish a Catholic community. Fr. Schramm laid a stone symbolizing the intent to build a church and Catholic parish. Through the contributions of 33 people, a small frame church surrounded by gorgeous oak trees was built on the newly purchased acre and a half. It was a mission of St. Martins.

Dedication of the new church was held on October 22, 1890. On January 31, 1891, an additional parcel of land was acquired and six years later, a school was established with a lay teacher in charge. St. Michael was established as a parish in 1916. A new rectory housed a resident priest possibly until the early 1930s when the parish was closed for several years. It is believed that it was reopened about 1934 and Fr. Bruemmer from St. Peter in Jefferson City came for Mass.

Through most of the parish history, administrators, usually from St. Peter's or priests from LaSalette Seminary in Jefferson City, served the parish. In September 1962, Fr. Norman J. Ahrens, from St. Peter was appointed administrator. In 1968, under his leadership, the building now used as the parish center was built. The parish closed in February 1970. Through the faith and hard work of the Catholic community led by an interim Parish Council, St. Michael was reopened on December 24, 1984.

Groundbreaking for a new church was held on December 24, 2000. Christmas Eve Mass was celebrated in 2001 in the unfinished church building. This also marked the anniversary of the reopening of the parish in 1984. In March 2002, members gathered in the parish hall and proceeded to the new completed church building for Mass. The dedication was on June 23, 2002, with Bishop John R. Gaydos presiding.

St. Michael, Russellville

St. Anthony, St. Anthony
1906

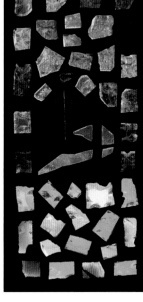

Early members of the Catholic church in St. Anthony traveled long miles to worship in St. Elizabeth. But in 1906 Fr. Bruch and community volunteers poured the foundation for the first church in the new parish named to honor St. Anthony of Padua. Because the parish lacked a resident pastor, priests from Brinktown, Vienna and St. Elizabeth journeyed to St. Anthony to offer Mass.

In 1908 Fr. C. Strausberger took charge of the parish. In 1909 a rectory was built with donations and volunteer labor by the parishioners.

❧ *First church built in 1906-1907*

In 1954 construction began on the present church building, which was dedicated on September 4, 1955. St. Anthony congregation has grown over the years and is proud of its heritage of community involvement through donations of personal time, material goods and money.

❧ *Stained-glass window portraying the cross*

St. Anthony is blessed with the presence of its elders, but also enjoys the energy and enthusiasm of many young people who comprise the community today.

Located in beautiful, rural mid-Missouri, St. Anthony of Padua celebrates 100 years as a parish in 2006.

❧ *Sanctuary of the first church*

❧ *Intérior of St. Anthony Church*

❧ *St. Anthony, St. Anthony*

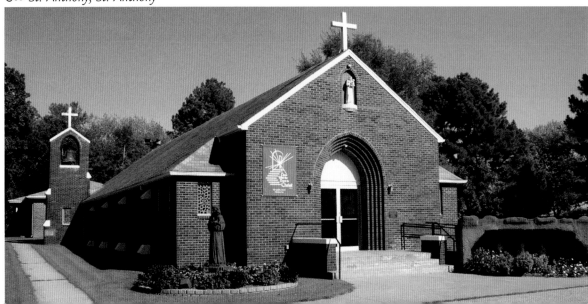

🐦 *Interior of St. Clement Church*

St. Clement, St. Clement
1871

St. Clement parish originated on August 11, 1871, when the Most Rev. Peter Kenrick, Archbishop of St. Louis, obtained 10 acres in Pike County, "on the premises" of which "there shall be erected a Catholic church to be known as the St. Clement Church," as the County Recorder of Deeds stated. Before then a mission church had been erected in New Hartford to serve the Catholics already settled in Pike County. Some have said that the Rolla parish served it until it was placed under St. Clement's jurisdiction in 1884.

As the number of German Catholic settlers grew, Clement Grote's home was used for church services, with the Franciscan fathers of Quincy coming once a month. The first church was completed in 1873 at a cost of $2,000. Fr. Charles Brockmeir was appointed the first pastor on November 18, 1882. In about 1883, the first St. Clement School was started, and in 1884, the first rectory went up.

By 1897 the German community had outgrown their first church. Under the direction of Fr. Aertker, a new church of Gothic design, costing $10,000, began with the laying of the cornerstone on August 18, 1897. It was dedicated on May 11, 1898. Fr. William Fischer, who was substituting for Fr. Henry Minges recuperating from an accident, helped bring electric power to the community. Upon Fr. Minges' return, a new school building was erected in 1924. Besides classrooms, it provided living quarters for the sisters. St. Clement celebrated its Golden Jubilee on October 2, 1923.

During the pastorate of Fr. James Bresnahan beginning in 1947, a winter chapel was installed in the school, along with other improvements. The following year the old church was renovated when Fr. Thomas Odlum became pastor in 1948.

Succeeding pastors continued to add to the complex: a Community Center and a credit union. 1955; a new school, 1961; a new rectory in 1964; the present church on October 19, 1969; and a parking lot and school lunch program, 1974.

In subsequent years many new programs and projects were introduced: St. Clement Charities, kindergarten classes, weekly Bible classes and information forum, a pre-school, a Sunday school program, the Renew Program, the Journey in Faith Program, a Kenneth Jones Tracker Pipe organ, and in 1985, the Adoration Chapel.

St. Clement celebrated its 125th anniversary on Saturday, November 23, 1996.

The parish of St. Clement is anticipating an early learning center for pre school age children and is in a planning stage for a multi purpose building (parish offices, classroom, meeting rooms, gymnasium).

🐦 *St. Clement, St. Clement*

St. Lawrence, St. Elizabeth
1871

🙠 *Interior of St. Lawrence Church*

German immigrants erected a small frame church in old St. Elizabeth in 1870. When the town was relocated, a large frame building dedicated to St. Lawrence served for worship until Bishop Lillis of Leavenworth laid the cornerstone of a new church in 1905. The church was formed of 400,000 bricks made on the property of clay drawn from a clay pit on the church grounds.

Ten years later a magnificent pipe organ was installed.

In 1929 when Fr. Frederick Brauch died, closing 29 years of dedicated ministry in St. Lawrence, some 80 priests graced his funeral with their presence. More than 50 priests attended the parish's centennial celebration in 1972, Bishop Michael McAuliffe officiating.

The vibrant spiritual energy of the parish is reflected in the fact that it has given 2 priests and 12 sisters to the service of the Church.

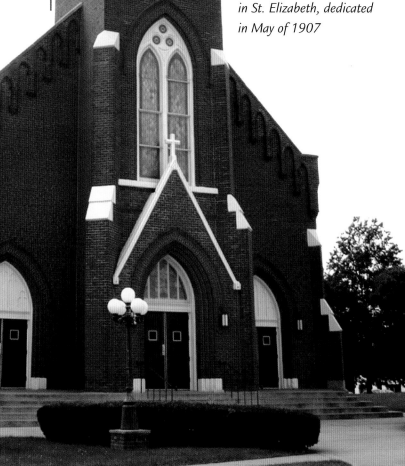

🙠 *St. Lawrence Church in St. Elizabeth, dedicated in May of 1907*

Immaculate Conception, St. James
1870

꩜ *Immaculate Conception, St. James*

German Catholic immigrants began to arrive at the Meramec Iron Works by way of Ohio from 1830 to 1850. Many Irish Catholic railroad workers also settled in and near St. James. In 1868 Immaculate Conception Church was officially established and is the oldest church in the community of St. James. Fr. Francis P. Gallagher was the first priest assigned by Archbishop Peter R. Kenrick of the Archdiocese of St. Louis.

The first church building was completed in 1869 and dedicated in 1872. In 1872 land was purchased and was consecrated as a cemetery.

In 1898, a colony of Italians settled in Rosati, then called "Knobview." The influx of Italian speaking new members in Immaculate Conception was so great that language became a problem. In 1906, Archbishop J.J. Glennon assigned Fr. Ottavio Leone to serve the

St. James and Knobview Catholics. In 1906, Fr. Leone initiated construction of a church and rectory in Knobview, now a separate parish of St. Anthony's in Rosati.

In 1955, under the leadership of Fr. Raymond Rau, a new church was constructed and on November 6, 1960, Bishop Joseph M. Marling of Jefferson City dedicated it.

Immaculate Conception community has been blessed by the spiritual guidance of many pastors.

꩜ *Interior of Immaculate Conception Church*

St. Martin, Saint Martins
1885

❧ The first school

❧ Interior of the church

❧ St. Martin School today

F ounded in 1885 to serve a largely German immigrant population, St. Martin parish continues to be a strong, vibrant faith community dedicated to serving the Lord and one another as well as the broader church.

Parishioners have shown a deep commitment to providing quality Catholic education to the children. The one-room schoolhouse that

opened in 1888 has been transformed over the years to the current complex, which serves 220 students. In addition to their strong support of Catholic education, St. Martin faith community members continually strive to build and strengthen spiritual and social ties that bond the diverse and faithful members together.

❧ School children vacation Bible School

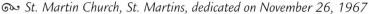

❧ Catechetical Lesson

❧ St. Martin Church, St. Martins, dedicated on November 26, 1967

St. Patrick, St. Patrick
1839

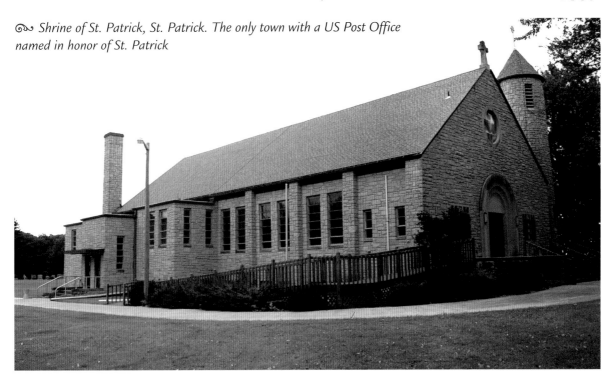

👉 *Shrine of St. Patrick, St. Patrick. The only town with a US Post Office named in honor of St. Patrick*

St. Patrick began as a simple log church in the southern portion of Clark County in 1834 and was served by Jesuits until 1846, when a resident pastor was named. A brick church was subsequently built in 1860, but was later replaced by a frame church in 1903. The school connected with St. Patrick opened in 1910 and was administered by the dedicated Sisters of Divine Providence. Later the Sisters of St. Francis carried on as the educators in the school.

When Fr. Francis O'Duignan came to the parish, he was the driving force behind the building of the current Shrine of St. Patrick, which was dedicated on March 17, 1957. The Shrine is famous for its Celtic architectural style and for its stained-glass windows made in Dublin, Ireland.

A yearly festival is held at the Shrine on March 17, the feast of St. Patrick, and there is a long-held tradition of a Fourth of July gathering that continues to this day.

👉 *St. Patrick honored in stained glass with triple St. Patrick Cathedrals*

St. Robert Bellarmine, St. Robert
1941

In June 1942, early into World War II, Fr. Herman Schuessler came from Dixon to celebrate Mass with a few Catholics assembled in the old Waynesville Theater. From these humble beginnings was built the first concrete block church structure in 1951. Cardinal Ritter of St. Louis, inspired by the first name of Fr. Robert Arnold, dedicated the Church to St. Robert Bellarmine, the 16th century cardinal, theologian and patron of catechists. The building was erected on Route 66 and from this church the city of St. Robert took its name.

The Altar and Rosary Society formed in 1957. In 1963, Fr. Charles Pfeiffer became the first resident pastor, creating an independent parish, and the Knights of Columbus established a local council. The current building, first used in 1964 and dedicated on May 2, 1965, is east of the old church. Resurrection Cemetery was added in 1969, the rectory in the 1970's and the St. Gregory Pavilion in 1995.

≈ Interior of St. Robert Bellarmine Church

In 1992, St. Jude in Richland was adopted as a mission community. Today, St. Robert Bellarmine is the faith home of more than 250 families. Funds are being raised for an Education and Multi-Purpose Building to meet the current and future needs of the parish.

≈ St. Robert Banner

≈ St. Robert Bellarmine, St. Robert

St. Thomas the Apostle, St. Thomas

1869

🕊 *St. Thomas the Apostle, St. Thomas*

St. Thomas Parish recognizes its beginnings with the first missionary visit of Fr. Ferdinand Helias, S.J. in 1838. Masses were celebrated in family homes when Fr. Helias would visit. The first registered baptism took place in 1841. The first parish church, a log church, was constructed in 1848 at Indian Bottom Settlement. A frame church replaced this church in 1851. In 1856 the parish church and presbytery were relocated to the present church property in St. Thomas.

🕊 *Interior of St. Thomas Church*

The parish was served by priests out of the Mission Center at Westphalia until 1869 when St. Thomas the Apostle Church became an independent parish and Father Aloysius Mayer was appointed the first pastor.

The parish's first school was erected on parish property in 1874. The present church was completed and dedicated on October 22, 1884. In 1939 the beautiful mosaic windows were installed and miraculously survived the 1948 tornado that demolished much of the church property. The parish rebuilt and restored the parish buildings. A gym was added atop the parish hall in 1969, which completed the present parish buildings. The school at St. Thomas became a part of the Cole R II public school district in 1962, but when the public school pulled out in 1989, the parish community decided to begin again with a Catholic School of the parish property. Early in 2000, the parish began looking into expanding the present parish school and hall to meet the growing needs of the parish activities and school.

On May 1, 2005, ground was broken on the expansion, which will add three classrooms to the school, a new library and computer lab, a school office and a new parish hall. The motto of the expansion reflects the development of the parish and community of St. Thomas, which is "Branching into the future" in faith.

🕊 *Stained-glass window of Jesus teaching*

🕊 *Window portraying Jesus with the little children*

St. Joseph, Salisbury
1870

Interior of the church

Stained-glass window of the Holy Family

St. Joseph Church, Salisbury

St. Joseph School

The first movement to organize a congregation for the Catholic people of Salisbury, Missouri, was made in 1870. In 1874 Fr. M. Busch, a pastor at Glasgow, Missouri, induced the Salisbury congregation to build the first Catholic church edifice in Salisbury. It was a frame structure situated about a quarter mile northeast of the present church site.

In 1890 Fr. John L. Gadell became the first resident pastor for Salisbury. Under his leadership the present church site was purchased. A school building and convent were erected on the southwest corner of the property in 1891.

In 1896 Fr. John Hennes succeeded Fr. Gadell to undertake the building of the rectory. When Fr. Joseph F. Lubeley took charge on September 1, 1903, the frame church was no longer adequate. On July 4, 1904, the cornerstone of a new edifice was laid.

The church, built of native sandstone, is one of the few rock churches in Missouri. On July 10, 1905, the congregation assembled for the first service in their house of worship. It was dedicated on November 16, 1905.

Interior of Sacred Heart Church

Sacred Heart, Sedalia
1882

The first Sacred Heart Church, rectory, school and convent were built by Fathers of the Society of the Most Precious Blood from Ohio in October 1882. Then the parish primarily served German immigrants who had previously belonged to St. Vincent, Sedalia. Sisters of the Congregation of the Precious Blood from Dayton, Ohio, taught in the school.

Until 1902 the Precious Blood Fathers who lived at Sacred Heart also served missions in Lexington, Clifton City, Cole Camp, Versailles, Gladstone, Eldon, Houstonia, Cross Timbers, Higginsville, California, Cedron and La Monte.

In 1891 work was begun on the present church building. It was dedicated on April 20, 1893. A school was built across the street from the church in 1906 and in 1909 a convent was added. A new rectory had to wait until 1925. By the fall of 1944 the school included grades 9 to 12. In 1956 the property was enlarged on the north end and a new school wing was built on it. By 1958 the grade and high schools enrolled 520 students. In 1962, the parish included 2200 families and 650 in the school. Today the school is using another classroom wing and a new gymnasium.

In 1984, the church underwent its first renovation. Currently the original building is being restored to its pre-1980 state.

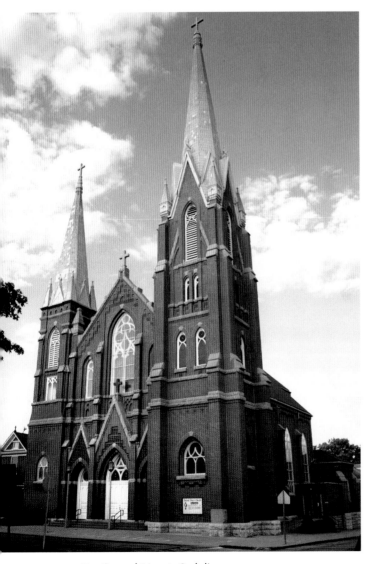

Sacred Heart, Sedalia

Sacred Heart School

St. John the Evangelist, Bahner
1845

St. John the Evangelist parish began in 1838 when a group of German Catholic families settled in the southeast corner of Pettis County. Religious needs and instruction were met in gatherings in homes of members of the community, with occasional visits by priests from Jefferson City and Westphalia.

In 1848, the first church was erected and served as a focal point for prayer meetings and monthly Masses by itinerant priests. A parish school was also built in 1859. These buildings served the community until 1881 when the present church was built in what is now Bahner, three and one half miles northwest of the original site. A parsonage was constructed at the same time and the old church was moved to the location to serve as a school until 1923 when it was torn down and replaced with the present school building. The rectory was completed in 1931 at which time two Benedictine sisters took up residence in the old parsonage to provide religious and educational instruction for the nearly 50 children attending school. Today the old parsonage is gone and the rectory is abandoned.

Presently St. John Catholic Church is a mission of Sacred Heart parish in Sedalia. Services are held every Saturday evening and CCD classes meet on Wednesday nights. The parishioners are proud that their parish has been in existence for 167 years and is still actively bringing the word and the sacraments to its people.

St. John the Evangelist, Bahner; Mission of Sacred Heart, Sedalia, dedicated on May 29, 1919.

Statuary of St. Patrick, church patron

St. Patrick, Sedalia
1866

Interior of the church

The first church in Sedalia, St. Vincent, was built in 1865. A rectory was attached the following year. Sedalia was a growing community and so a new church was finished in 1875, also with an attached rectory. The Sisters of St. Joseph staffed a private school in 1881. They lived in a convent on 4th and Washington.

By 1902, when the old church was declared unsafe, a new church was begun across the street. It was dedicated to St. Patrick, acknowledging the many Irish families who came to town to work on the railroad. At this time the Bishop of Kansas

City declared Ohio Street the boundary between Sacred Heart on 3rd and Moniteau and St. Patrick. German immigrants were to attend Sacred Heart and Irish Catholics, either St. Patrick or Sacred Heart.

St. Patrick church building was not dedicated until September 25, 1910. The present rectory was built in 1922 and the new school followed in 1924. It closed in 1969.

In 1981 the Society of the Precious Blood took charge of St. Patrick. Since then the Fathers have been sharing programs and staff between the two parishes seven blocks apart. Until 2003 St. Patrick Church served a mission at St. Joseph, Clifton City. The present church was remodeled in 2003.

St. Patrick, Sedalia

St. Mary, Shelbina
1879

Many of the 160 households which make up the present St. Mary's congregation trace their ancestry to the Catholics of Maryland who migrated westward. Preserving their faith through the wilds of pioneer life in Kentucky, they came to settle claims in Monroe and Shelby County, Missouri and establish a church in the new land. One pioneer whose descendants account for nearly one-third of the present membership of the church was Mrs. Susan Beaven Gough McAtee.

Priests from Macon and Indian Creek tended the needs of Shelbina Catholics until 1878, when Fr. James O'Reilly, a young priest, was appointed pastor. Soon after he came, the need of a church building became evident. Early parishioners who helped finance the building of the first church, completed in 1879, were J.W. Towson, John Thomas, William Ridge, John McAtee, James H. Gough, George B. Gough, Clem Hamilton, James Worland, James Hardy, Joseph Jarboe, Jack Melton, Al Bowling, George Greenwell, Robert Bell, Ben Gough, Edwin Worland, John Worland, Louis Hale, Mrs. Lewis Saunders, Mrs. Gabie Combs, and Mrs. Sydney Taylor. The church was named St. Mary's in honor of the Mother of Christ.

During the pastorate of Fr. E.A. Casey (1884-1889) a rectory was purchased, and five acres of land in the southeast part of the city of

Interior of St. Mary Church

Shelbina was bought for a cemetery. Catholics of Irish descent arrived in the late 1800's. The Riley, Hurley, Kelly, Lillis, and Powers families were among these.

Fr. Bernard Luebbering became pastor in 1954. Fr. Leo Buhman came as an assistant in 1955 and was later named pastor, serving until 1969. A large church hall built on newly purchased property east of the present church was named "Father Buhman Center" in honor of the pastor who had planned and worked to see it built. Monsignor Joseph Bugler was named pastor in the fall of 1969 and served until 1988.

Since its organization in 1903, the Altar Society has held regular meetings. The Knights of Columbus Council received its charter in 1921. An annual parish event is the turkey dinner, served in November each year.

St. Mary, Shelbina, dedicated on May 13, 1924.

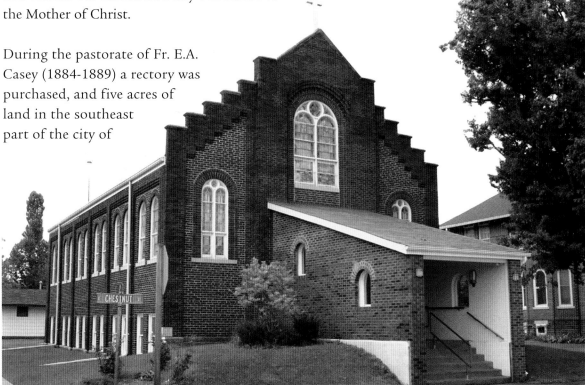

St. Joseph, Slater
1882

In the fall of 1877 the Catholic families of Slater were able to participate in Mass in their hometown. That first Mass was celebrated in the Chicago and Alton railroad station house with Fr. John T. D. Murphy, the pastor of Marshall's Catholic church, officiating. In May 1882, T.B. Blackstone, president of the Chicago and Alton Railroad, donated the site where the present church is located. On March 13, 1883, a new church was completed and dedicated as St. Joseph Catholic Church under the pastorate of Fr. Edward Ryan. The parish then consisted of about 25 families. The first Mass in the present parish church was offered on Easter Sunday 1926. It was dedicated on May 15, 1927, by Bishop Lillis.

In 1971 the sanctuary was renovated in accordance with the directives of Vatican Council II. In 1986 a new ramp-entrance made the church accessible to people of all ages. The interior of the church was renovated in 1999.

Since its beginning, the parish has had 20 pastors. Four parish members chose religious life: Fr. David Maher and Srs. Joseph Theresa Kruse, Frances Louis Borges and Anna Marie Himmelberg.

ॐ *St. Joseph, Slater*

St. Michael, Steelville
1949

☙ *St. Michael, Steelville*

S t. Michael's Parish was organized in 1949 by Fr. Joseph Boland. The first Mass was celebrated in the summer of 1949, attended by fourteen families in the County Courthouse in Steelville.

September of 1949 a building was purchased and remodeled. September of 1950 it was dedicated. The Ladies Guild was formed in January of 1951. The CCD was formed in September of 1974.

In the summer time when the area drew a lot of tourists to float the area streams, stay at the resorts and camp grounds, St. Michael would overflow out on the streets and people would stand at the windows to hear Mass.Realizing that the church space was becoming inadequate for Sunday Mass, a building fund was started. Another property was purchased in January of 1983 and remodeled. November of 1992 ground was broken for additional worship area and dedicated on June 13, 1992.

The hard work of our dedicated past leaders, parishioners, priests and pastoral administrators has made St. Michael a great parish to be part of and a wonderful place to worship. We are a true family parish and welcome visitors to Mass and activities.

We are growing in faith and a lot of activity. Our younger parishioners are more involved in their parish.

We are all thankful to our Lord for the many blessings he has bestowed upon our Parish Family of St. Michael.

☙ *St. Michael, Steelville*

St. Francis Xavier, Taos

1838

In the summer of 1838 Fr. Ferdinand Helias, S.J, came to the area now known as Taos to care for the spiritual needs of German immigrants. There were only 20 families gathered when he celebrated Mass for the first time on May 28, 1838.

Soon 10 acres were purchased from the Haar family to be used for a church and school. In 1840 the first church, a simple log structure was built and dedicated to St. Francis Xavier, renowned Jesuit missionary to the Far East. The community was known as Haarville until the soldiers returned from the war with Mexico and began to call the town Taos.

The second church, made of stone, had the distinction of being the first stone church built in the interior of the state. Its cornerstone was laid on April 6, 1944.

❧ Interior of St. Francis Xavier Church

On the morning of August 11, 1874, the "Apostle of Central Missouri" was found dead in the churchyard. Legend has it that he died while ringing the Angelus. Fr. Helias was buried in the parish cemetery. In 1964 his body was moved to the church and reinterred.

It was under the direction of Fr. John Guender in 1881 that plans were made for the erection of a third church. The old rock church had become too small for the growing parish. The present church was finished in 1883 at a grand cost of $9000. It was dedicated to the honor and glory of God.

❧ Memorial plaque of the founder of several area parishes

❧ St. Francis Xavier, Taos

St. Andrew, Tipton
1857

St. Andrew parish, Tipton, was established in the 1840s with services held in a log Church situated where the parish cemetery is today. The present Gothic Church in the center of town was dedicated on May 24, 1884. St. Andrew Church is well known for the beautiful stained-glass windows depicting the glorious and joyful mysteries of the rosary and the large Stations of the Cross placed between the windows.

St. Andrew parish has 389 registered families and 126 students enrolled in grades one through eight.

For more than 60 years St. Andrew's parishioners have worked together to host the annual parish Thanksgiving Day dinner and festival.

Members of the Parish Council, Altar Society, Knights of Columbus, PTO and Youth Group represent only a few of the parishioners helping St. Andrew's grow.

🕮 *Interior of St. Andrew Church*

🕮 *St. Andrew, Tipton*

Sacred Heart, Vandalia
1891

The Catholic Church in Vandalia had its beginning in February 1891 when five families gathered at the first service held in the home of John Frazier Coontz. Fr. Edward J. Dempsey, who resided in Mexico, Missouri, served the area from 1891 to 1899. Fr. J. Dillon succeeded him from 1899 to 1912.

In the spring of 1913 a site was purchased at the southern end of the town and construction of the first church building was begun. Fr. Gilfillan of Jefferson City, who was assigned in February 1912 to serve the various missions in northern Missouri, is credited with providing the guidance necessary finally to complete the building process, and Mass was offered in the newly constructed church in October 1913.

Window dedicated to the Immaculate Heart of Mary

After 1915 Fr. Patrick Lyons resided in Laddonia and attended the mission in Vandalia monthly. He was replaced after six months by Fr. H. J. Schlueter who resided in Laddonia and made monthly, then weekly, visits to serve the Catholics of Vandalia.

With the completion of the Walsh Fire Clay Brick Plant came an influx of Catholic families. In 1920 Fr. Schluetter was ordered to move his residence to Vandalia where he became pastor

Interior of Sacred Heart church

in 1920. Following several more pastors and the formation of the new Diocese of Jefferson City, in 1956 construction began for a nine-room rectory and expanded the church's seating capacity to 250.

A new church was completed and dedicated on December 3, 1978 by Bishop McAuliffe.

Subsenquently a marble altar, lectern, tabernacle table, stained-glass windows and padded cushions for pews were installed and plans were formed for a new parish center. It was completed in September 1991. In that same year a shrine of the Blessed Mother and the Sacred Heart was dedicated in memory of all the past priests of Sacred Heart.

Through faith the parish has deepened its understanding of community and together the people have grown spiritually, financially and socially.

Sacred Heart, Vandalia

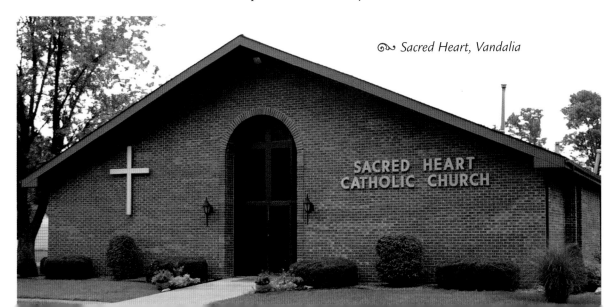

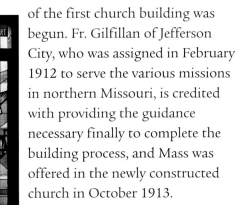

St. John, Laddonia
1889

The Louisiana Purchase, 1803, was the remote cause of Laddonia becoming an organized township. For centuries Laddonia and environs could have been called the Land of the Tall Grass—six to eight feet tall. It was not until the advent of the steel plow that the land could be tamed.

❧ *The Good Shepherd pictured above the entrance*

In the early days of 1840 to 1884 came "greazers," then "feeders" and finally cultivators. Following the charter of the North Missouri Railroad Company in 1851, Laddonia was founded in 1871. The first Catholics bought acreage in its southern portion.

St. John Catholic Church had its inception in 1877 when Fr. O'Leary, then resident pastor of the Catholic parish in Mexico, first visited the mission. For some years Mass was offered either in a schoolhouse or in a rented hall. Then Archbishop Kenrick bought two lots at the corner of 7th and Elm Streets to be used as the site of Saint John Church. They paid $40 for both lots and the church cost $715 to build.

After Fr. O'Leary's pastorate, Fr. Edward J. Dempsey, pastor of the parish in Mexico, made monthly weekday mission trips between the years 1878 and 1899. Under Fr. Joseph Gilfillan, the rectory was built at the Laddonia parish in 1912. At his death, the mission received its first resident Catholic priest, Fr. Patrick Lyons. The next pastor, Fr. Henry Schlueter served

Laddonia along with Vandalia and Rush Hill. With the prosperity of the World War era and the erection of the new $1 million Walsh Fire Clay Brick Plant at Vandalia, it was evident that a resident priest would be required. After three years, Fr. Schlueter moved his residence to Vandalia. Subsequent years saw the parishes divided and reunited.

In 1936 under Fr. James Klein's pastorate at St. John, the beautiful shrine of our Blessed Mother was erected on the church grounds. A number of pastors served both communities until under Fr. John Walsh the leaning church building was demolished and a new structure erected in 1987. A new shrine replaced the old in 1990.

In 1992, St. John and the surrounding community formed a food pantry to serve needy families. It distributed food from the parish hall section of the church until

❧ *Shrine of the Blessed Virgin Mary on the church grounds, St. John*

December 1994 when a separate building to facilitate food distribution was constructed.

❧ *St. John, Laddonia; Mission of Sacred Heart, Vandalia*

Visitation, Vienna
1867

Visitation, Vienna

Interior of Visitation Church

Maries County and Vienna, its county seat, came into existence in 1855. The first Catholic church, a 40-foot-long log structure, was built at the north end of Vienna on four acres. The land was donated to the St. Louis Archdiocese by Thomas Anderson and his wife, Myra Wiseman Anderson, wealthy Protestants who owned a working plantation in the area.

The log church, named St. Mary, was partially destroyed by fire in the 1860s. Jesuit priests from Westphalia, principally Fr. John Goeldin, made missionary visits until a new church was constructed.

In 1867 John Felker, a son-in-law of Anderson, allowed a Catholic church to be built on lots he owned in Vienna. Felker also donated 10 acres west of Vienna for a town cemetery. Five acres were reserved for Catholics and five for Protestants.

A third church as well as a rectory was constructed on the Felker lots in 1885. Recently remodeled, the rectory still stands.

Fr. John Fugel arrived in 1896 to begin a 40-year pastorate. Planning an even larger church, he purchased a concrete block-making machine and had the parishioners cast the blocks. In addition to their labor, they were expected to bring the needed sand and gravel. Fr. Fugel worked alongside the men to keep the blocks coming. The wooden 1885 church was razed and a new cornerstone was set in 1907. The church was dedicated in May of 1910.

The block-making machine was also used to construct visitation Interparish Catholic School in 1926. This school building also housed and is still used today by the office for Fr. Fugel's newspaper, "The Home Advisor".

Fr. Fugel is said to have owned the first automobile in town and strung a telephone line from Brinktown to Vienna. He ran a movie theater in the church basement. As projectionist, he could put his hand over the lens and censor any scenes he deemed objectionable. This good priest died of a stroke in 1936.

Visitation parish currently shares its pastor with Guardian Angels, St. Aloysius, and St. Boniface parishes.

Window of Jesus with the Eucharist

St. Stanislaus, Wardsville
1880

ᕫ *Interior of St. Stanislaus Church*

St. Stanislaus parish was established in 1880 and St. Stanislaus School in 1882. Catholic education has always been a centerpiece of this beautiful Catholic parish located in Wardsville. Throughout the late 1800s and early 1900s, classes were taught in both the English and German languages to meet the needs of the large number of immigrants from Germany.

The hilly, wooded village of Wardsville reminded the German immigrants of their homeland. Prayers were also recited in both languages, thereby enabling some to act as interpreters for those who knew only German.

Since then, St. Stanislaus has grown to more than 600 families and a K-8 school population of more than 300. A native daughter who entered the Sisters of Providence was Sr. Bernarde Winkelmann, now deceased.

ᕫ *St. Stanislaus, Wardsville, dedicated June 28, 1925.*

St. Ann, Warsaw

St. Ann, Warsaw
1945

Bishop O'Hara of the Diocese of Kansas City dedicated St. Ann Catholic Church on Sunday, March 3, 1946. The first Mass was celebrated by Fr. Urban Landoll of the Society of the Precious Blood. St. Ann was then a mission of SS. Peter & Paul parish, Cole Camp.

In May 1946 St. Ann became a mission of the Catholic church in Windsor with priests of the Society of the Precious Blood continuing to serve when St. Ann became part of the newly formed Diocese of Jefferson City in 1956.

Too small to meet the needs of a growing parish, the original building went through several modifications between 1956 and 1966.

Ten years later, St. Ann was officially established as a parish.

A modern rectory adjoined the church, which was completely remodeled in 1979. A new parish hall was dedicated in 1984. The parish membership was 7 families in 1946, 30 in 1950 and 160 in 1985. The first Altar and Rosary Society was founded in 1946, the first Parish Council, in 1978 and the Knights of Columbus received their charter in 1984.

St. Ann church sanctuary decorated for Christmas

From 1989 to 1992, began the building of a new church. Fr. Dennis Schaab saw the completion of the project.

Mortgage-burning celebration in 2003.

SS. Peter & Paul, Cole Camp
1878

SS. Peter and Paul parish in Cole Camp dates from 1878. In 1880 Cole Camp became part of the newly established Diocese of Kansas City. The original frame church was replaced in 1913 by a larger brick structure to accommodate the growing membership of Bohemian and German immigrants. In the 1970s Cole Camp became a mission of St. Ann in Warsaw, and it has shared the spiritual leadership of pastors from the Society of the Precious Blood since 1956.

In 1987 parishioners were faced with the task of rebuilding the deteriorating 70-year-old church. The new church and fellowship hall, dedicated on September 18, 1988, is on two donated acres at the west edge of the city. Parishioners and local artisans performed much of the work on it.

Recently SS. Peter and Paul held a 125th Anniversary celebration with visitors, former pastors and parishioners from all over the country in attendance. A most important lesson was learned.

Although worship structures may surround them, the people are the Church.

SS. Peter & Paul, Cole Camp; Mission of St. Ann, Warsaw

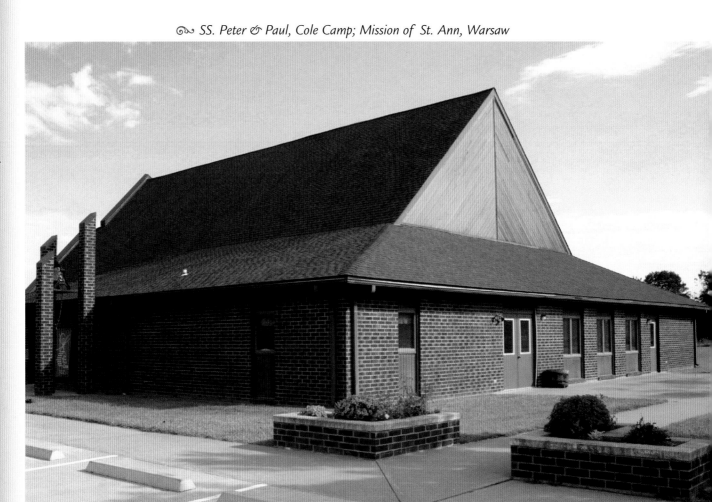

🕮 *Interior of St. Joseph*

St. Joseph parish, the oldest German Catholic parish west of the Mississippi River, celebrated its first Mass on August 6, 1835. The present church was built in 1848, dedicated on October 24, 1894, with a bell tower added in 1883. A major renovation in 1905 elevated the church and added stained-glass windows.

As German immigrants placed a high value on education, a school was established in 1837

and has continued to the present day. It is the oldest school in the diocese.

Because of the church's significance as a visual, social and intellectual landmark in the Westphalia community, it was Placed on the National Register of Historic places in 1972.

🕮 *St. Joseph, Westphalia*

🕮 *Quilters of the St. Anne Sewing Circle*

🕮 *Largest Collection of Sacred Relics in Diocese of Jefferson City*

St. Mary of the Angels, Wien
1876

꩜ *Immaculate Conception Mission Church at Hamden*

꩜ *Interior of St. Mary of the Angels Church*

꩜ *Living Stations of the Cross*

꩜ *Our Lady of Perpetual Help Shrine, St. Mary*

S t. Mary of the Angels parish in Wien is more than 125 years old. Built in 1876 by the Franciscans as a Monastery, the parish was given to the secular clergy in 1914. St. Mary's was one of ten churches in the diocese to be designated as a Pilgrimage Site for the Jubilee Year. For several years members of the parish portrayed the Living Stations of the Cross on Palm Sunday. At times more than 30 area churches were represented. Share and care is known far and wide for their charity work. A youth choir has been organized.

꩜ *St. Mary of the Angels, Wien, dedicated October 4, 1892*

Mary Immaculate, Kirksville
1886

Mary Immaculate Parish was founded in 1886 as a mission of St. Mary parish in Adair to serve the people who traveled to Kirksville for medical treatment.

Fr. O'Shea, pastor of the Adair parish (established in 1876), celebrated Masses in Kirksville's Masonic Hall until the first Mary Immaculate Church was completed in 1892. The pastor attributed the success of the establishment of both the parish and the church facility to John L. Porter of Kirksville. Interesting, Porter wasn't Catholic!

The first church was built for $3,400. A number of gifts, such as a crucifix and a statue of the Sacred Heart, were given to the church by grateful patients of Dr. A.T. Still, but most of these were destroyed during a cyclone on April 27, 1899.

Kirksville's first Catholic church after the Cyclone of 1899

In 1905, St. Louis Archbishop John J. Glennon dedicated a new church on the present site. That church burned down in 1945. Mass was celebrated in Washington School until the present church was completed in 1947. Mary Immaculate School opened in 1956. Religious teachers included Sisters of St. Francis, Sisters of Charity of the Incarnate Word, and Sisters of Mercy of County Langford, Ireland. In 1968, the school became the first in the diocese to be staffed by lay teachers.

Mary Immaculate in 1928

There are now 125 students in grades K-8. Parish organizations and ministries include: Altar & Rosary Society, Knights of Columbus, Young at Heart seniors group, Quilting circle, Ministry of Care to the homebound, choir and liturgy, Interchurch ministerial alliance, social outreach to people in need, RCIA, religious education, parent support, sacramental preparation, youth ministry, prayer line and Bible study. Kirksville pastors also serve St. Rose of Lima parish in Novinger, and continued to serve the mother parish in Adair as a mission until 1972.

Present church, dedicated in 1945

Kirksville Newman Center, built in 1990 and expanded in 2000

St. Michael the Archangel at St. Joseph, Edina

Religious Orders

🙠 *Ascension window at Holy Guardian Angels, Brinktown*

Society of Jesus

The Society of Jesus (commonly known as the Jesuits) was founded by St. Ignatius Loyola and seven of his students in Paris in 1534 for the purpose of fostering spiritual perfection, Church renewal and apostolic service to God through zealous service to the Pope.

The first Jesuit priests in the United States arrived in 1805. Jesuit Father Charles de la Croix presided at the first recorded Mass in present-day Callaway County, Mo., in 1819. A Flemish Jesuit priest named Father Ferdinand Helias D'Huddeghem traveled from St. Louis to Osage County in April 1838. Headquartered first in Westphalia, then in Haarville (now known as Taos), Fr. Helias visited 11 Missouri counties — an area larger than his native Belgium — establishing Catholic parishes and missions. He founded St. Peter parish in Jefferson City and the parishes in Taos, Loose Creek, Rich Fountain, St. Thomas and Cedron, and occasionally visited such communities as Boonville, Pilot Grove, Columbia and Sedalia. He is remembered as the "Apostle of Central Missouri." Rich Fountain's and Linn's first resident pastors were Jesuit priests. From Westphalia, Jesuit priests served such parishes as Koeltztown and Vienna. Jesuits were founding pastors in Montgomery City and present-day Starkenburg. Jesuit priests from St. Charles were among the first to offer Mass for Catholic settlers in present-day Indian Creek, Center, Palmyra and elsewhere in northeastern Missouri in the 1820s and '30s.

Congregation of the Missions

The Congregation of the Missions (the Vincentians, also known as the Lazarists), founded in 1625 by St. Vincent de Paul, has a long association with the Church in Missouri. The Vincentians' primary charisms are working with the poor, and forming seminarians into priests. Bishop Joseph Rosati, founding bishop of the newly created Diocese of St. Louis (1829) was a Vincentian, as were the founders of St. Mary of the Barrens near Perryville (1818), a school to which Saint Louis University and Kenrick-Glennon Seminary trace their lineage. Bishop William DuBourg of the Louisiana Territory and the Floridas invited Vincentian priests, brothers and seminarians from Rome to the United States in 1815. Vincentian Father Walter J. Reisinger has been pastor of the Dixon and Crocker parishes for almost a quarter-century.

☙ *Madonna and Child painting at Bishop's residence*

Order of Friars Minor

The Order of Friars Minor (Franciscan priests and brothers), established by St. Francis of Assisi in the twelfth century, served parishes in the present-day Jefferson City diocese for over 125 years. The order, founded in the 1100s for the purpose of prayer and preaching, established a friary at St. George parish in Hermann in 1875, as well as parishes and missions in Berger, Little Berger, Morrison, Chamois, Rhineland, Starkenburg and Hancock Prairie. From the Friary of St. Mary of the Angels in Wien, Franciscan priests and brothers staffed the parishes in Wien, Brunswick, Hurricane Branch, Indian Grove, Hamden, New Cambria and Lingo from 1876-1914. From Quincy University in Quincy, Ill, Franciscans have supplied help to the parishes in the northeast section of our diocese, and members of the order served as chaplains at the old St. Francis Hospital in Marceline.

Missionaries of La Salette

The Missionaries of La Salette were established in 1852 for the purpose of spreading the Blessed Mother's message — given in an 1846 apparition to two children in La Salette, France — of prayer, repentance and atonement for the world's sake. They serve in North America, South America, the Philippines, Europe, Africa, India and Madagascar. The La Salette Missionaries established a minor seminary in the heart of Jefferson City in the 1950s. From there, they formed future priests for the missions and conducted Catholic retreats, in addition to ministry in nearby parishes and St. Marys Health Center. Although the seminary closed in 1968 and was sold several years later, La Salette Father Clarence Wheeler, former rector of the community, has continued to serve for many years at Carmel. Father Arthur Lueckenotto, a Meta native, is a La Salette missionary serving in Madagascar.

☙ *Stained-glass window of the Virgin Mary at Mary Immaculate Church, Kirksville.*

Congregation Of The Missionaries Of The Precious Blood

The Congregation of the Missionaries of the Precious Blood (Precious Blood Fathers) is a society of apostolic life of priests, brothers and students. St. Gaspar del Bufalo founded the society in 1815 in present-day Italy to renew the clergy and laity through devotion to the Precious Blood Christ offered up at the Last Supper and shed during His saving passion and death. Over time, the society developed an emphasis on the interdependent pillars of mission, community and spirituality. The first Precious Blood priests and seminarians arrived in the United States in 1843 to serve in parishes and schools. In the Jefferson City diocese, Precious Blood fathers have served as pastors in Sedalia, Bahner, Warsaw, Cole Camp, Fayette, Pilot Grove, Clifton City, Boonville, California, Cedron, Marshall, Sweet Springs, St. Elizabeth and other communities. Before his elevation to the episcopacy in 1947, Bishop Joseph M. Marling C.PP.S., the diocese's founding bishop, served two terms as provincial general of the society's American Province. The society had 314 members in North America in 2000.

Order of St. Benedict

St. Benedict of Nursia in the early sixth century established twelve monasteries near Mount Subiaco in modern-day Italy for the purpose of promoting a life modeled closely after that of the early Christians as revealed in Scripture. St. Benedict's Rule and the order that would adhere to it spread throughout Europe and beyond. In 1873, at the invitation of an Irish missionary named Father James Power, Prior Frowin Conrad and Adelhelm Odermatt of Engelberg Abbey in Switzerland were sent to northeastern Missouri in 1873, where they opened a novitiate and in 1881

ᕓ *Window of the Wedding Feast at Church of Risen Savior, Rhineland.*

built a monastery. The novitiate eventually became Conception Seminary, now known as Conception Seminary College. While remaining faithful to their call to community life and prayer, adherence to the Rule of St. Benedict, and the operation of the seminary, the monks of Conception also have been doing parish work for 130 years. They currently serve 15 parishes in five states, including St. Lawrence parish in St. Elizabeth, and within this decade have served in Mexico, Canton, LaGrange, Kahoka and St. Patrick. Father Daniel J. Merz of the Jefferson City diocese is an instructor at the seminary college.

De La Salle Christian Brothers

The De La Salle Christian Brothers are part of the international Institute of the Brothers of the Christian Schools, which has been educating young people since its founding in 1680 by St. John Baptist de La Salle. The Brothers and their colleagues sponsor universities, high schools, middle schools, retreat centers and a variety of other educational ministries. Students of Helias Interparish High School in Jefferson City are among the more than 900,000 young people served by the Christian Brothers worldwide. Christian Brothers have been on the staff since the school opened in 1956, and at one time maintained a residence nearby.

Franciscan Brothers Of The Holy Cross

The Congregation of the Franciscan Brothers of the Holy Cross was founded by Brother James Wirth in 1862 in Trier, Germany, in order to help the poor, the sick and the suffering and willingly respond to the needs of the time. Their formation and daily existence rest on three pillars: religious life, vocational activity, and the experience of community. Members of the congregation served the Seminary and the parishes in Canton, LaGrange and St. Patrick in northeastern Missouri during the 1980s and '90s.

Window of the Wedding at Cana at Risen Savior, Rhineland.

The Diocese of Jefferson City has been blessed by the presence of dedicated women religious since before its establishment as an independent diocese. They educated generations of Catholics in the faith, tended the poor, the aged and the infirm, served in various ways in parishes and diocesan offices and functioned as an arm of the bishops in caring for the flock.

School Sisters of Notre Dame

The School Sisters of Notre Dame were among the first to come to the diocese in 1866. Founded by Blessed Theresa of Jesus Gerhardinger in Bavaria in 1833, the original sisters educated poor girls.

To serve the needy and German immigrants, the sisters came to the United States in 1847, and in 1866 at Westphalia, Central Missouri. They ministered in schools, orphanages and schools for children with special needs. Before 1952, the sisters taught in public schools in half a dozen cities and towns of the Jefferson City Diocese. Over the past 50 years alone, 570 sisters have ministered in 54 localities in the diocese, serving in schools, diocesan administration, as DREs and in social services. Today 22 sisters continue to respond to the needs of women, youth and the poor in the diocese.

Sisters of the Most Precious Blood of O'Fallon

A group of young women from Baden, Germany — led by Mother Theresa Weber — gathered in Steinerberg, Switzerland in 1845 to form a contemplative congregation for the purpose of promoting Christ fully present in the Most Precious Blood in the Blessed Sacrament and to educate young people. Political persecution led them to the French Alsace, where Germans weren't allowed to teach. Some of the sisters remained and took up an exclusively contemplative life; some went to Gurtweil, Germany, to pray and teach. The latter moved to Belle Prairie, Ill., in 1870, during the German Revolution. Of those, some moved to St. Louis and eventually started an independent congregation in O' Fallon, Mo. They continued teaching, establishing schools and enhancing the liturgy with music and art.

By 1906, they were already working in 10 areas of the present-day Jefferson City diocese. Since then, 293 sisters have served in education, prison, Hispanic and pastoral ministries in 19 towns and cities in the diocese. Members currently serve in Boonville, Columbia, Jefferson City, Lake Ozark, Sedalia, Macon and Unionville. Precious Blood Sisters of the Dayton, Ohio, province taught in Sedalia.

ꝏ *Jesus with the children of the World*

Sisters of Divine Providence

Founded as a congregation by a German bishop and a French noblewoman in 1851, the first Sisters of Divine Providence were Mother Marie and five others who were dedicated to the education of rural girls and care for the sick and the poor. After the repressive laws of Bismarck, the sisters made their way to the States in 1876. Since 1932 more than 125 sisters have served in five areas of the Diocese of Jefferson City. Today, besides their work in the United States, the sisters minister in Korea, Peru, China, Poland, Spain, Puerto Rico and Santo Domingo.

Sisters of Charity of the Incarnate Word

More than 100 years ago in 1890, the Congregation of the Sisters of Charity of the Incarnate Word came to Jefferson City to carry out apostolates in health care and teaching. Founded in France, they were established in Texas in 1869. Over the century, within the Diocese of Jefferson City they have served in some 10 cities and towns. The Sisters of Charity of the Incarnate Word also operated hospitals in Sedalia up to 1930. Today, besides the United States, they minister in Mexico, Peru, El Salvador, Guatemala and Zambia. Today laywomen who are so inclined join in the charism and ministry of the sisters as lay associates. Another form of membership is being a lay missionary of the Incarnate Word who commits several years to carrying on the mission of the congregation to actualize the saving and healing love of the Incarnate Word by promoting human dignity.

Dominican Congregation of Our Lady of the Rosary

The sisters of the Dominican Congregation of Our Lady of the Rosary were founded in 1876 by Alice Mary Thorpe who responded to needy women and the sick in New York, New York. The congregation established its motherhouse in Sparkhill, New York, expanding its ministry to include teaching. In 1902 the sisters were invited to teach in Monroe City where Holy Rosary School has had a Dominican principal for 133 years. They also served the Shrine of St. Patrick, St. Patrick.

☙ *Window of St. Elizabeth of Hungary*

Benedictine Sisters of Our Lady of Peace Monastery, Columbia

Branching out from a Benedictine monastery in Fort Smith, Arkansas, the Benedictine Sisters of Our Lady of Peace monastery in Columbia came to the Jefferson City diocese in the 1960s when the Fort Smith sisters were already teaching in three parishes of the diocese and operating St. Joseph Hospital in Boonville. Nine years later the monastery in Columbia became independent, but it wasn't until 1995 that they inhabited a new monastery. The sisters follow the rule of St. Benedict—Pray and Work—by reciting the Liturgy of the Hours three times a day, spending time in spiritual reading and meditation and engaging in apostolates such as directing religious education in parishes, prison ministry, ministry to the homebound, counseling, spiritual direction and giving retreats. One of their foremost characteristics is hospitality.

Sisters of Charity of Leavenworth

Followers of St. Vincent de Paul, St. Louise de Marillac and Mother Xavier Ross, the Sisters of Charity of Leavenworth have focused on serving marginalized people for more than 150 years. In 1858 sisters from Nashville reached out to the Territory of Kansas to care for the poor, teach, tend the sick, care for orphans and visit prisons. In 1978 they came to the Diocese of Jefferson City where over the years eight sisters have served in seven cities. Today the congregation ministers in education, health care, social services and pastoral ministry in the Midwest and western U.S. and in northern Peru.

Sisters of St. Joseph of Carondelet

The Sisters of St. Joseph of Carondelet is part of a congregation of religious sisters founded by six women under the guidance of a Jesuit priest in 1650 in LePuy, France. They dedicated their lives to the apostolate of completive prayer and to "exercise all of the spiritual and corporal works of mercy of which woman is capable and which will most benefit the dear neighbor." At St. Louis Bishop Joseph Rosati's request, they established a convent in Carondelet, now part of St. Louis, in 1839, bringing with them almost two centuries of apostolic zeal and educational traditions. Since 1984 they have served the people of Appalachia and the Jefferson City diocese. Today CSJ sisters serve in 40 states and in Peru, Japan and Chile. They operated the former St. Elizabeth Hospital in Hannibal, and currently serve in parish ministry in Columbia.

St. Cecilia graces many choir lofts in the diocese

Sisters of Christian Charity

Although the Sisters of Charity came to St. Peter, Fulton, in the Diocese of Jefferson City in 1992, they have a long history. The congregation was founded by Pauline Mallenckrodt in Westphalia, Germany, in 1849 to care for neglected children and the blind. Under Bismarck's persecution, they came to New Orleans in 1870, and in one year were ministering in 13 missions in 5 states. Their first motherhouse in Wilkes-Barre, Pennsylvania, was moved to Wilmette, Illinois, between 1913-1916. In 1927 the province divided into east and west branches, the western province encompassing seven states, including the Diocese of Jefferson City where they engaged in teaching, after-school care, visiting the sick, pastoral and youth ministries and other parish functions. Today they serve in six countries and the mid-, south and east U.S.

Franciscan Sisters of Our Lady of Perpetual Help

The Franciscan Sisters of Our Lady of Perpetual Help who minister in the Jefferson City diocese are an offshoot of the Joliet Franciscan Sisters of Mary Immaculate. Arriving to serve the Polish immigrants at St. Stanislas Kostka in St. Louis, the sisters who came in 1901 were originally known as the Polish Franciscan School Sisters of St. Louis. Soon the community gained enough members to branch out to rural Missouri and Illinois, making St. Louis their headquarters from 1907 to 1957. The sisters operated schools all over the country, including African-American, Hispanic and Indian children in their ministry. In 1953 they began to work in hospital care in Ohio and Tennessee. In 1960 they opened a mission in Thailand. In 1990 the sisters sold their motherhouse to live simply in convents, homes and apartments. Today 124 sisters serve the poor and empower those they meet with hope and joy. One of their members, Sr. Boniface Dyrde, was cured through the intercession of Blessed Junipero Serra. Two sisters currently minister in the diocese.

Sisters of St. Francis of Oldenburg, Indiana

Franciscan Sister Theresa Hackelmeier in 1851 traveled from her convent in Vienna, Austria, to the frontier town of Oldenburg, Ind., to start a religious congregation to teach the German-speaking children and care for orphans. The sisters who joined her established schools throughout the surrounding area and eventually in neighboring states. Since then, their work with children has been expanded into higher education, parish work, missionary endeavors, and assisting Native American communities in southwestern United States, thus helping to carry out the Catholic Church's vital mission to spread the Gospel. The pastoral minister in Brookfield, formerly of Russellville, is a member of this congregation. Sisters also have served in St. Clement and Rolla.

Sisters of St. Francis of Lafayette, Ind., established and staffed St.George School in Hermann.

Franciscan Sisters of Mary

The Franciscan Sisters of Mary arrived in St. Louis with their foundress, Mary Odila Berger, in 1872. The Sisters of Mary's mission was to live a consecrated religious life while helping the sick and injured. At first helping the sick, orphans, mothers-to-be and young working women in their homes, the sisters began to build and staff hospitals. In 1894, several SSMs, guided by Sister Mary Augustine Giesen, committed themselves to a Franciscan way of life and formed the Sisters of St. Francis of Maryville. Monsignor Otto J. Hoog of St. Peter parish in Jefferson City visited the Sisters of Mary in St. Louis in 1903 and asked them establish a hospital in central Missouri. The sisters went door to door in the Capital City, seeking donations for the project. They opened what is now St. Marys Health Center in Jefferson City in 1905. For years, the sisters operated the hospital as nurses and administrators, and several remain on the St. Mary's staff. The two branches of the original community were reunited in 1987 to become the Franciscan Sisters of Mary. They also served in Marceline.

☙ *Flight into Egypt, Shrine of St. Patrick, St. Patrick*

Order Of Mount Carmel

The Order of Mount Carmel (Discalced Carmelite nuns), a cloistered, contemplative order founded by St. Teresa of Avila in the 1600s, has maintained an intensely prayerful presence in the diocese since 1960. Carmelite nuns live in tightly cloistered communities, seeking out a life of divine intimacy with Christ through a regimen of simplicity, discipline, unceasing prayer, and contemplation in solitude, all in imitation of the Blessed Mother and for the spiritual well being of the Church and the world. Forsaking distractions from the outside, the sisters are free to give themselves completely to God. The first foundation of the Carmel in the United States was made in 1790 in Baltimore. Bishop Joseph M. Marling, C.PP.S. in 1960 invited the Carmelite nuns from the monastery in Santa Fe, N.M. to begin a new monastery in Jefferson City. Mother Mary Teresa, who had established the Santa Fe monastery in 1945, arrived with six other sisters during the Easter Season of 1960. Their present monastery near the Cathedral of St. Joseph was completed in 1962. "The prayers and sacrifices of these good sisters will bring us many graces and heavenly favors," Bishop Marling stated.

Carmelite Sisters Of The Divine Heart Of Jesus

Venerable Mother Maria Teresa of St. Joseph, a native of present-day Poland who joined the Catholic Church at age 33, founded the Carmelite Sisters of the Divine Heart of Jesus (Carmelite DCJ) in 1891, after experiencing a vision of two mighty brown ships -- one larger than the other – chained together. She understood the vision to be a call from God to combine apostolic service and charity with the contemplative prayer of the cloistered Discalced Carmelite nuns. The order she founded in Holland began serving the needy, homeless, migrants and the unchurched in Europe. She arrived and her sisters began establishing homes for the elderly and for orphans in the United States in 1912. Monsignor Joseph Vogelweid of St. Peter parish in Jefferson City in 1948 asked members of the order serving in Kirkwood, Missouri, to establish a home for elderly Catholics in Jefferson City. With the American provincial's permission, the sisters established St. Joseph Home for the Aged in Jefferson City. Carmelite DCJ sisters operated the home from 1950-2005, during which time they and the rest of the staff cared for hundreds of people.

Adorers of the Blood of Christ

Established in 1834 by Maria DeMattias in Aculto, Italy, "to be a reconciling presence to the poor in our midst" and to be a living image of the divine charity with which Christ shed His Blood, Adorers of the Blood of Christ of Ruma, Ill., served the diocese from the 1970s into the 1990s, mostly in administration and religious education. Sister Kathleen McGuire ASC served in Catholic campus ministry in Jefferson City before accepting a position as a missionary in Liberia, where she completed her life as a martyr for Christ.

Sisters Of Mercy

Mother Catherine McAuley established the Sisters of Mercy in 1831 in Ireland and opened the first convent in 1835. The principal aims were "to educate poor girls, to lodge and maintain poor young women who are in danger... and to visit the sick poor." The congregation spread across Ireland and England and into the United States during the 19th century. Monsignor Francis O'Duignan — a native of Co. Longford, Ireland, and an early pastor of St. Joseph parish in Jefferson City — invited Sisters of Mercy of Swinford, Ireland, to help him establish St. Joseph School in 1960. The first group of sisters arrived with their provincial, Rev. Mother Clare, later that year. Sisters of Mercy from Swinford also would become teachers and administrators at St. Stanislaus School in Wardsville. Sisters of Mercy of Ballymahon, Co. Longford, would teach and administrate at Columbia Catholic School in Columbia, and Mary Immaculate School in Kirksville. Sisters from Sligo served at Cathedral until 1990.

¦ *Agony in Garden at St. Joseph Church, Edina*

School Sisters of St. Francis

The School Sisters of St. Francis is an international congregation of women religious established in 1873 by Mother Alexia Hoell, Mother Alfons Schmid and Sister Clara Seiter -- who were Franciscan sisters from Schwarzach, Germany -- in Wisconsin "to witness to the Good News of Jesus Christ and the presence of the reign of God as we enter into the lives and needs of people, especially those who are poor." Among the more than 1,200 current members is a sister living in Brookfield and doing prison ministry in nearby Chillicothe.

Congregation of Sisters of the Third Order of St. Francis

Franciscan Sister Theresa Hackelmeier in 1851 traveled from her convent in Vienna, Austria, to the frontier town of Oldenburg, Ind., to start a religious congregation to teach the German-speaking children and care for orphans. The sisters who joined her established schools throughout the surrounding area and eventually in neighboring states. Since then, their work with children has been expanded into higher education, parish work, missionary endeavors, and assisting Native American communities in southwestern United States, thus helping to carry out the Catholic Church's vital mission to spread the Gospel. The pastoral minister in Brookfield, formerly of Russellville, is a member of this congregation.